Finding Hope

Real Stories. Real Steps. Real Peace.

Hope Blankenship

Finding Hope

Copyright © 2025 by Hope Blankenship

All rights reserved.

Scripture quotations, unless otherwise noted, are taken from the Holy Bible, New International Version®, NIV®. Copyright © 1973, 1978, 1984, 2011 by Biblica, Inc.™ Used by permission. All rights reserved worldwide.

Cover design by Hope Blakenship

Interior design by Hope Blankenship

ISBN: 9798292231004

Printed in the United States of America

Dedication

Daniyel,

Thanks for your support and love - for the patience and for standing by me, even in the moments when I felt hardest to love.

To Austin, Grace and Addison

What a blessing and a joy it is to be your mom. Each of you carries a special light that reflects the heart of God. I'm so grateful that you love the Lord and walk in His truth. You all lead with strength, compassion, and a deep love for others that leaves a mark on everyone you encounter. I may not show it often enough but know this—I love each of you to the moon and back, and I'm so proud of who you are and who you're becoming in Christ.

"I have no greater joy than to hear that my children are walking in the truth." — 3 John 1:4

NanaMac,

There aren't enough words to describe the profound impact you've had on my life. Your faithful prayers and unwavering love for the Lord are the greatest gifts I've ever received. I truly believe your battle-worn prayers helped save my life. Thank you for loving me right where I was and always allowing me to be fully me.

Family and Friends ,

Each of you has encouraged, supported, and loved me in your own way. You hold a special place in my heart. Thank you for walking this journey with me and for being a beautiful part of my life.

Table of Contents

Preface

From Ruins to Roots - My Journey to Hope

Hope is not just a concept—it's a lifeline, a deep-rooted assurance that there is meaning in the waiting, purpose in the struggle, and light beyond the present darkness. It's often quiet, sometimes fragile, but always powerful. For some, hope feels strong and steady; for others, it's something they're still trying to find. I've always carried a sense of hope—it's been part of me for as long as I can remember. (Funny enough—it's part of my name, so I didn't have much choice!) But over time, I began to see that hope isn't just something we hold onto—it's something we can live from. It has the power to shape how we see ourselves, how we move forward, and how we walk through the everyday moments of life.

I never doubted God's presence. I had a deep sense that He was real and with me, even in the hardest moments. But I didn't always feel like I was walking closely with Him—not in a way that shaped my daily thoughts, emotions, or choices. On the surface, I kept going—doing what needed to be done—but something inside felt distant. I had learned how to function, how to appear strong, but there were parts of me that felt disconnected and unfinished. I was functioning physically but had not yet discovered the deeper, fuller life that God offers. What I didn't see then was that God was already at work, shaping a story I hadn't yet learned to trust—or believe I was meant to tell.

And then I found myself standing on holy ground, quite literally—Tel Dan, Israel, 2023.

The picture on the cover of this book is more than an image; it's a turning point. It's a visual memorial of the moment I truly believed that I would write this book—not as a joke, not as a vague idea that hovered just beyond reach, but as a calling etched into my bones.

Tel Dan—this ancient city in northern Israel—is a place most tourists skip past quickly. But to me, it was where heaven reached down and whispered, *"This is where your story changes."*

Biblically, Tel Dan was both a symbol of compromise and a marker of identity. After the kingdom of Israel split, King Jeroboam erected a golden calf here, trying to create his own path to worship apart from Jerusalem (1 Kings 12:28–30). It became a place of false worship, of broken alignment with God.

And yet, that's what makes it so powerful: God still speaks from broken places.

This ground, once tainted by idolatry, now holds one of the strongest archaeological confirmations of Scripture—the Tel Dan Stele, where the words "House of David" are etched in stone, affirming the legacy of a king after God's own heart. That juxtaposition—failure and faithfulness, rebellion and redemption—is the very tension this book lives in. It's the tension I lived in for years.

I had always joked about writing a book. Friends would laugh and say, "You *have* to write that down!" But their comments hit a wall inside me—a wall of unbelief. I didn't trust my voice. I didn't believe that anything I had to say would matter, much less help someone else. That self-doubt was my own version of the false altar: a belief system I had built, not God.

But God, who calls us by name, doesn't let us remain bound to counterfeit truths—not even the one that whispers we're too broken to be used.

Over time, He began placing me in conversations I couldn't ignore. People, unprompted, would tell me again and again, *"You need to put that in a book."* Their words were like water on a seed that God had planted long ago—words that began to push against the hard surface of my doubt. First a tiny sprout broke through. Then, as He nurtured it with truth, community, and confirmation, it grew. A bush. Then a tree. And now—

what I believe is an oak of righteousness (Isaiah 61:3), rooted in grace and bearing fruit for others.

This book is that tree. And Tel Dan is the soil where it took root.

Israel changed everything. My 2023 trip wasn't just a vacation—it was my pilgrimage. A journey not just through land, but into truth. It transformed my vision of the world, reshaped how I understand people, and redefined my perspective on America... but above all, it revolutionized how I see myself. It was as if I walked the same footsteps as ancient prophets and patriarchs, and in doing so, I found a connection with God so personal, so sacred, that I knew I could never go back to the way things were.

At Tel Dan, God met me in the ruins. And not just the ruins of that ancient city—but the ruins within me.

If you're holding this book, maybe you've known ruins, too. Maybe you've stood in places where belief and doubt wrestle. Maybe you've been buried under the weight of fear, shame, or a story you're too afraid to tell. My prayer is that as you turn these pages, you'll find the same voice that found me among the stones: the voice of Hope. Not the shallow kind, but the kind that holds your gaze steady when everything feels like it's falling apart. The kind that says, *"Even here, even now—I am not finished with you."*

Because God is still restoring what's been broken. Still planting oaks of righteousness where ashes once lay. Still calling us out of compromise and back into covenant. And yes—He's still crafting redemption stories from the very places we once deemed beyond repair.

Welcome to mine.

And perhaps... the beginning of yours.

Chapter 1

When Peace Comes in the Dark

Nighttime was the hardest. Sitting on the bed, cuddled under the feather blankets with a classic comfort movie playing low in the background, the baby in her bassinet, within arm's reach, my Bible lying next to me and my pictures app opened on my phone. I scrolled through the days, weeks, months, and years of memories of my husband, Daniyel and me. Memories of places we ate, dates we went on, babies we had, birthdays we celebrated, trips we took, and most of all, the ones of just the two of us.

It was 2017, and tensions were high between Korea and the U.S. The news reported daily on the escalating pressure between the nations, particularly from North Korea. Normally, I wouldn't have paid much attention, but this time was unique—Daniyel was serving a 12-month remote tour in South Korea with the U.S. Air Force. He had been on deployments before, overseas and to "the desert," but this one felt different, more frightening. He had left just 30 days after we welcomed our third child into the world—a baby girl. When he left, it felt as if our hearts had been ripped from our chests, and joy would not return until he did.

As I lay in bed one night, a few months into the deployment—sleep-deprived, lonely, and worn thin by the grind of it all—fear settled over me, slow and heavy, like a fog that wouldn't lift. The news murmured in the background, reporting another distant threat, and my thoughts drifted to Daniyel. I imagined his voice on our next call, casually mentioning the daily "exercise," the one where they suited up in gear to rehearse for chemical warfare, as if that kind of terror could ever be routine. I missed him so much it ached. The weight of the day, the week, the month—all of it—finally broke through, and I cried, hot tears spilling silently in the dark.

The news had become a relentless drumbeat of fear—daily reports of North Korea testing rockets, often without warning and alarmingly close to South Korean borders. Though the two countries were not at war, the unpredictability of these missile launches created a steady undercurrent of tension. Each update blurred into the next, the frequency increasing until it felt like a constant presence in my life. It was as if I could hear the phone ringing in the distance, a phantom sound warning me of a visit I prayed would never come.

Sitting there in my bed, darkness outside, my mind became my worst enemy, painting vivid images of uniformed officers standing at my door, their faces heavy with sorrow, their eyes cast downward as they prepared to deliver the news that would shatter my world. The thought sent me spiraling. My mind grasped at answers that didn't exist. How could this be happening? What if he didn't come home—what then? Where would I go with this life we built? Where would the kids and I live, how would I make it work? How do you hold a family together with a broken heart? How do you look your children in the eyes and speak the unthinkable out loud?

I couldn't bear the weight of those questions. Suddenly, the fear tightened around me until I felt like I couldn't breathe. Overcome with emotion, I cried out, my voice breaking, "Lord, please, just show me! I can't take not knowing! Let me face it now and know instead of waiting for that moment."

It was all I could do—to plead with God for an answer, for a glimpse of hope, for anything that would tell me Daniyel would come home to us safely.

Then, suddenly, my tears stopped, and a peace entered the room, settling around me. I felt as if a hand covered mine, and a voice whispered, "No matter what happens in this season, whether he comes home or home to me, I will see you through, I will be with you, I will carry you, and I will never leave you."

I took a deep breath and felt it all rush in and fill my lungs. When I exhaled, it took with it the weight I had been dragging for weeks. At that moment, I understood what it meant to lay it all down. People say, "Lay it at the feet of Jesus," but that day, I didn't just hear the words—I felt them. I lived them. I grasped what it meant to release the fear, the questions and the control I never really had in the first place.

Life is uncertain. It always will be. But that's where faith begins—when everything else feels like it's falling apart, and the only thing left to hold onto is the One who never does. I had to surrender the worry, the ache, the endless 'what ifs' to the One who says, "Come to Me, all you who are weary and burdened, and I will give you rest.

Take my yoke upon you and learn from Me, for I am gentle and humble in heart, and you will find rest for your souls" (Matthew 11:28-29)

Tears of relief followed, this time not from fear, but from the release of it. The tension I had carried for months finally loosened its grip. I knew then that the Lord had heard every cry, every whispered plea in the dark, and had held each tear in His hands.

"You keep track of all my sorrows. You have collected all my tears in your bottle. You have recorded each one in your book" (Psalm 56:8).

I didn't receive a promise that Daniyel would come home alive, no clear voice or certainty about the future—but I had peace. And in that peace, I knew God had met me in the depths of my brokenness and exhaustion, not to give me the answers I wanted, but to give me Himself. Hope flickered back to life in me. The road ahead would still be hard, the unknown still real— but I knew who held every step of it in His hands.

What are you carrying right now that needs to be laid down? What weight have you convinced yourself you must bear alone? He's already reaching for it. You only need to let go.

Deployment and Challenges

The reality of military life is sobering. Nearly three out of four active-duty spouses have endured deployments lasting more than 30 days, and 92% report experiencing significant stress and anxiety during those separations (Blue Star Families Survey, 2023). The strain doesn't end with homecoming—an overwhelming 97% of military divorces occur *after* a deployment ends. One in four military spouses faces depression (National Military Family Association). But in the middle of all this weight, one factor consistently makes a difference: community. Studies show that strong social support increases a spouse's ability to adjust to deployment separation by 24% (Orther & Rose, 2006). In the chaos and crisis that so often comes with military life, it's not just about surviving—it's about who walks with you through it.

Six months into Daniyel's deployment, I decided to remodel our detached garage into an office for my growing bookkeeping business. With a new baby, the demands of work, and the weight of solo parenting, I needed the space—and a project to help pass the deployment time. Thankfully, I wasn't completely alone. A young woman, Jen, from our church had moved in to help while Daniyel was away, stepping in as a nanny and supporting me with the kids and household duties. Her presence was a blessing I hadn't realized I would need.

A year earlier, Daniyel and I had purchased our "forever home"—three acres of quiet land where we planned to raise our family. It was everything we'd dreamed of.

Seven months into his year-long assignment in Korea, on April 14th, I came across news of a severe rainstorm just north of us. Minor river swelling was expected in our area, but it didn't seem alarming. Our home sat ten feet above Katrina's flood levels, and while a nearby creek occasionally spilled over, it had never been a serious concern.

That Sunday morning, I woke to water slowly creeping across the road and reaching the end of our long driveway. It wasn't the first time, but this time the current was deeper and moving faster. Because of a low spot at the driveway's end, the water was too high to drive my car through. A neighbor kindly came to pick us up in his truck and took us to church. We expected the water to recede by the time we finished, just as it always had before.

After church, the water hadn't gone down—in fact, it had risen, creeping closer toward the house. Still, I took the kids to a birthday party in a nearby city that afternoon. Within the hour of being there, I checked our home security camera—and saw the water had reached the front door. Then suddenly, the feed went dark.

The power had cut out. The water had reached the outlets inside. My heart dropped.

Our dog was still inside, kenneled on the first floor. Panic set in.

A whirlwind followed - friends took my kids, we made calls and searched for a boat to rescue our dog Molly, and I rushed back to find our entire neighborhood street flooded by a fast, dangerous river. Neighbors on the other side texted, coordinating efforts to get to the house but the water was moving too quickly to be able to navigate getting back there safely. As I waited behind a friend's SUV near the neighborhood entrance for a firefighter friend to arrive with a boat, one of my pastors called.

"How are you feeling?" he asked.

For the first time in hours, I paused, took a deep breath, and tears spilled over. "I don't know. Just pray."

Our firefighter friend, Luke, and the nanny, Jen—who absolutely loved Molly—took a boat back toward the house to try to get to her. On the way, they ran into some neighbors from the other side of the road who'd heard Molly was stuck inside. Those neighbors had already brought their own boat, broken a window, and gotten her out safely. After Luke and the nanny made sure Molly was okay, they headed back by boat to the main road to fill us in on the house—and just how much water was everywhere.

Daniyel had always been my rock, my defender, and my personal superhero. As a career firefighter, he was my automatic first call whenever something went wrong—whether it was a real emergency or just me panicking over a spider in the house. Of course, more often than not, he'd answer the phone just to remind me (with a bit of good-natured annoyance) that he wasn't on duty 24/7 and definitely not the one to call instead of 911 in an emergency. But old habits die hard, and whenever life threw me a curveball, he was my call. Now, thousands of miles away, I had no choice but to take a deep breath, put down the phone, and face this crisis solo.

Standing behind that SUV on the side of the busy road, watching the water rush past me below, I thought back to that night in my room when God had promised to carry me through this season and I was brought peace in that moment. A gentle reminder of Philippians 4:7, which reads *"And the peace of God, which surpasses all understanding, will guard your hearts and your minds in Christ Jesus."*

The Aftermath and the Power of Community

The following days were a blur—filled with insurance claims, scheduling adjusters, renting industrial fans, meeting with contractors, school drop-offs, planning meals, and figuring out where we were going to live. My neighbor, a skilled remodeler, and the trusted contractor who had just completed the garage project, stepped in right away to help. It was a blessing that I had just finished working with him—he knew the house, and he was able to get started immediately on the main home.

We had lost so much: our home, the newly remodeled garage-turned-office, and even my car. Everything had to be gutted— four feet of sheetrock stripped from every room in both the house and garage. It was overwhelming, but we had no choice but to keep moving forward.

For several weeks, our church family, local firefighters, and even my son's high school classmates showed up to help with demolition and cleanup. My dad flew in from Alaska for two full weeks, rolling up his sleeves and working alongside the crews every day. The principal at our kids' school had generously allowed high school students to volunteer during the school day for class credit, and they came eager to work—

hauling debris, tearing out sheetrock, and doing whatever needed to be done.

But it wasn't just the help—it was how it came. I didn't have to organize, schedule, or ask. People just showed up. Friends arrived early with coffee and gloves, ready to get to work. Others came later in the day with meals for the crew. My kids were picked up without me even having to ask, taken out for the evening so I could focus. There was always someone there — asking "What's next?" or "Where can I help?"

The fire department from Daniyel's base came for several days in a row, giving their time like it was second nature. Neighbors brought tools. Friends dropped off supplies. People came in waves—some familiar faces, some I barely knew—but every one of them showed up with open hands and willing hearts.

We were also blessed with temporary housing, meals, and financial support. Friends, family, and our church community surrounded us like a safety net. One financial gift even matched the exact cost of Daniyel's last minute plane ticket home—a detail that left me speechless.

It felt like God had whispered our needs before I could speak to them—and His people responded.

I remember lying in bed each night, making a list of the faces I had seen that day, ending with a heart full of gratitude. Though my body ached from labor and demo, I was overwhelmed by love and thankfulness. To this day I still review those lists from time to time remembering that season. I am able to recall God's grace and faithfulness each time I review the long list of people that showed up for us.

What about you? When life feels heavy or uncertain, what do you look back on to remember God's faithfulness? Do you have your own lists or journal entries that remind you of His goodness—of the people He sent, the peace He gave, the ways He showed up? If not, what would it look like to start one now?

Daniyel used all of his available leave to come home for a month, but because he was on a remote assignment, he had to return back to Korea. While he was home, his fire chief suggested he apply for humanitarian orders—a special exception that allows service members to return early due to extreme family hardship. As soon as he got back to Korea, Daniyel submitted the application. The waiting felt like an eternity, but finally, at the nine-month mark of his deployment, he was granted approval to come home—for good.

What we didn't know then was just how perfectly timed it all was. Before this deployment, we had been preparing for the possibility of another move—likely out of state—for the final stretch of his 20-year Air Force service. But because he was approved for humanitarian orders tied to the flood, it anchored him here for the remainder of his service. The assignment that should have uprooted us instead secured us right where we were, giving us the stability we so deeply needed.

Looking back, it was clear: even in the chaos, God was orchestrating every detail.

Faith and Restoration

There were days both in the deployment and the construction when exhaustion weighed so heavily on me that even lifting my arms, let alone my head, felt impossible. Yet, during this season, I discovered the true essence of community and the peace of God that surpasses all understanding. When our world was turned upside down—without a home, without a car, with a newborn, two older children, and a husband unable to be present—I still experienced true peace.

I remember a particular moment burned into my memory each time I reflect on this season. Four days after the flood, our first insurance adjuster visited, and he was astounded at how much work had already been done. "I have never in 20 years seen this much completed so quickly," he said. "How did you get all this done in 4 days?"

That was because of community—because of the relationships we had built long before tragedy struck. My children will never see servanthood the same way again. They witnessed what true family and community look like in that season, a life lesson no flood could ever wash away.

Looking back, I see how God's hand literally carried us through. EVERY need we had in that season was met and frankly was met far beyond any expectation I could have dreamed. It was never just about the flood or the deployment—it was about faith, surrender, and trust. When everything was beyond my control and I felt completely alone, I had no choice but to lean on the One who always remains in control. And time and time again, He has proven Himself faithful.

Chapter 2

From Treehouses to turning points

Psalm 34:18 "The Lord is close to the brokenhearted and saves those who are crushed in spirit."

My childhood was traditional in many ways. I had two younger brothers and an older sister. We grew up attending church, spending time with friends in home groups—a small group of church members who meet throughout the week to build relationships and learn more about God together—and going to a small Christian school. We lived in a middle-class neighborhood with a treehouse and a swing set in the backyard. Most nights, my family gathered around the dinner table to eat together.

Birthdays were celebrated at Chuck E. Cheese like every other '90s kid. Stockings were full on Christmas morning, and my dad took us sledding and built forts in the snow. My mom cooked dinner every night, and we gathered around the table like clockwork. My siblings and I would quietly hide the bites we didn't want under our napkins before making our polite excuses and slipping away. We enjoyed outdoor adventures and made home videos that I still watch and laugh at today. We took camping trips and fished in the Alaskan wilderness during the summer.

Looking back, as a child, I felt that life was rich and family was important. There was a sense of security that came with our routine. I believed in the permanence of our family, in the way that children assume their world is unchangeable.

Then came the day that shattered that picture in my mind and heart—an event that would change the course of my next twenty years.

It was a bright, blue-sky day. I was twelve. I was playing upstairs when my mom came up after finishing laundry. Midway up, I casually asked her when my dad would be home. He often traveled for work, sometimes gone for several days, but this time felt longer than usual.

She stopped mid-stride, looked at me in a matter-of-fact manner, and said, "He left. He moved out, and he won't be coming home." Then she continued up the stairs, putting the laundry away.

I remember facing this moment as an adult, feeling as if a movie had zoomed in on my face—the kind of scene where the director wants to capture the dramatic impact on the actor. In that instant, my childhood ended. I was no longer the carefree, go-with-the-flow kid I had been. The family unit I had known for twelve years was gone. There was no explanation, no follow-up conversation about what life would look like now.

The Absence of Conflict and Its Consequences

Up until that moment, I had never seen my parents fight. I don't remember disagreements or arguments—conflicts were quietly handled behind closed doors, as was common in their generation. So, when my dad suddenly left, it hit me like a shock I wasn't prepared for. Because I'd never witnessed conflict between my parents, I had no idea how disagreements worked or how they could be resolved.

Research shows that children who grow up without seeing any conflict often struggle with handling disagreements later in life. A study in the *Journal of Family Psychology* found that kids who observe healthy conflicts—where problems are talked through and resolved—develop better emotional skills and problem-solving abilities. On the other hand, children who never see conflict can find it much harder to navigate their own relationships.

I'm not saying every couple should argue in front of their kids, but the absence of any visible conflict left me unprepared. Since I never saw my parents fight, I also never saw them make up. To me, couples simply didn't argue. This misunderstanding shaped my expectations in relationships and led to many challenges I had to work through later—unlearning what I thought was normal and learning how to deal with conflict in a healthy way. I'll share more about this particular part of the journey in later chapters.

Living Outside of Time

Later in life, I learned that when a traumatic event occurs in a child's life and they are unable to process the pain, the brain can enter a state called dissociative amnesia. This is a coping mechanism in which the mind suppresses the memory of the event, creating a gap in recollection that may persist until the memory is triggered through therapy, additional trauma, or the development of healthy, protective relationships. Some people recover these memories later in life, while others never do, as confronting the pain can be overwhelming.

In the days after that moment with my mother, I learned the facts: my dad had taken the family motorhome and was living in a nearby RV park. I heard he wouldn't be coming back to the church he had served and belonged to for so many years. But knowing these things didn't bring clarity—it only made the confusion grow deeper, because no one explained why any of it was happening.

In the book *Changes That Heal*, by Dr. Henry Cloud I received clarity about that moment on the stairs. He explains that when a child loses a parent at a crucial developmental stage, they have no one with whom to work through adolescent struggles. He writes that parts of ourselves can get trapped in "bad time," remaining exactly as they were when the trauma occurred. In essence, my twelve-year-old self was frozen, standing outside of time, standing in "bad time," perpetually waiting for an explanation that never came.

That day, I became numb. Without realizing it, I shifted into self-preservation mode.

Lost in "Bad Time"

For the next few years, I mostly just existed. I don't have many clear memories of daily life during that time. I wasn't overwhelmed by emotions—I simply went through the motions of whatever was happening around me. Both of my parents were carrying their own loneliness, pain, and frustration in ways that shaped the household. My dad was quiet and thoughtful, never speaking ill of my mom, even though I could sense he was hurting. My mom, however, often expressed her anger more openly, and sometimes that frustration came out toward me, especially when I asked to see my dad.

The summer after my parents separated, when my aunt came to visit my dad, I asked my mom if I could stay with them for a while to spend some time with him. Instead of calmly agreeing, my mom packed up all my things, drove me to my dad's new apartment, and threw everything on his front porch. Looking back now, I understand that my mom's anger was a reflection of the deep hurt she was feeling—something called "displaced aggression," where pain and frustration get taken out on those closest and easiest to reach, rather than the real source of the pain.

As a child, this kind of experience can leave lasting effects—hurting self-esteem, causing emotional confusion, and shaping how we learn to handle conflict later in life. After that, I ended up living with my dad for several years, facing even more emotional challenges along the way.

Eventually, my dad remarried a kind woman who had several younger children, and we moved to an upscale part of town. That meant switching schools, making new friends, and adjusting to life in a blended family with four new siblings. While we generally got along, I often felt like an outsider looking in. Before my dad and his new wife married, there had been a physical confrontation between her and my mom—a moment that lingered in the background. I could sense that she held some blame toward me, which made her keep her distance. There were days when the weight of that unspoken resentment felt heavy and inescapable.

These transitions brought new challenges, but much of the pain and confusion from earlier remained unaddressed, shaping the complicated emotional landscape I had to navigate growing up.

Rebellion as a Coping Mechanism

As I entered my teenage years, the unresolved pain I carried started to show up in new ways—mostly through defiance and rebellion. Looking back, I realize I was just trying to cope the only way I knew how. Acting out gave me some sense of control in a life that felt unpredictable and overwhelming. I didn't have the words to explain what I was feeling—anger, sadness, confusion—so I expressed it through risky choices and a hardened attitude. I've since learned that this kind of behavior is common for kids who experience divorce or trauma. For me, it wasn't about being bad—it was about trying to survive emotions I didn't know how to process.

When I got older, I began questioning my dad about the divorce—though my questions were often more accusatory than inquisitive. I was trying to reconcile and confront the past trauma with understanding, but I went about it the wrong way. I simply didn't have the tools to communicate my questions effectively. This created tension with my dad's wife, and eventually, I was told to move out. By that time, my mom had remarried, and her life seemed to have settled down, so I moved in with her and her new husband.

Her new husband had lost his previous wife to cancer, and he was one of the kindest, most humble, and intelligent people I had ever met. He loved me, my mom, and my siblings. He brought stability—emotionally and financially—something we hadn't experienced in years. He brought peace and harmony to the household. But by then, I was 16 and doing things more independent in nature so I was more like a tenant in the home than a daughter.

There were no rules in this house, which suited my defiant and independent streak. I continued making unwise decisions, hanging out with the wrong crowds, and partying. I had no idea what the next few years would hold—both miracles and messes. But through it all, I would learn some of my most valuable life lessons.

Hope Deferred

Looking back, those turbulent teenage years were messy and painful, but they marked the beginning of a journey—one that taught me about resilience, identity, and ultimately, hope. The defiance, the questioning, and the mistakes were more than just rebellion; they were my way of wrestling with deep emotions and trying to make sense of a world that felt out of my control.

Scripture reminds us in Romans 5:3-4 (NIV): *"Not only so, but we also glory in our sufferings, because we know that suffering produces perseverance; perseverance, character; and character,* *hope."*
This truth became real to me over time. The pain and confusion weren't the end—they were the soil where perseverance and character could grow, and from there, hope could take root.

If you're reading this and carrying the weight of hopelessness, shame, or guilt because of your past, please hear this: your story is not finished. Whether it's the mistakes you've made, or the pain others have caused you—things that were out of your control—those experiences do not get the final word. God does. The broken places, the hidden wounds, the chapters you'd rather erase—none of them are beyond His reach. There is hope, even if you can't see it yet, because the God who sees you also heals, restores, and redeems.

God's grace is bigger than any failure, and His love meets us exactly where we are. In 1 Peter 5:10 (NIV), we are promised: *"And the God of all grace, who called you to his eternal glory in Christ, after you have suffered a little while, will himself restore you and make you strong, firm and steadfast."*

No matter how lost or broken you feel right now, restoration is possible. Healing begins the moment you allow yourself to believe that you are worthy of hope—that your past doesn't disqualify you from a future filled with purpose, peace, and joy.

My own journey wasn't easy. There were many moments when hope felt far away. But each step forward, no matter how small or uncertain, brought me closer to a deeper understanding: hope is not just a feeling; it's a choice—a lifeline to hold onto when life feels overwhelming.

So, if you're struggling today, I invite you to take that step with me. Let hope be the light that breaks through the darkness. Your story is still being written, and the best chapters may be yet to come.

Here are some practical steps you can take to start moving toward healing and hope today:

1. **Acknowledge Your Feelings**
   It's okay to admit when you're hurting, angry, or confused. Naming your emotions is the first step toward understanding and healing. Journaling can be a helpful tool to process what you're feeling.

2. **Seek Support**
   You don't have to face this alone. Reach out to trusted friends, family, or a counselor who can listen without judgment and offer encouragement. You do not have

to carry this pain everywhere you go. There is freedom in talking to someone else even if you don't know where to start or what to say. Just take the step.

3. **Engage with Scripture**
   Find comfort and guidance in God's Word. Meditate on verses like Romans 5:3-4 and Proverbs 13:12. Let these truths remind you that your suffering is not meaningless and that hope is coming.

4. **Practice Small Acts of Self-Compassion**
   Take care of yourself physically, emotionally, and spiritually. This might mean setting healthy boundaries, prioritizing rest, or doing something you enjoy. Healing often begins with kindness toward yourself, and that kindness is a reflection of God's heart for you.

5. **Choose Hope Daily**
   Hope is a choice, not just a feeling. Each day, remind yourself that your story is still being written and that healing is possible. Simple affirmations or prayer can help reinforce this mindset. Write them down and tape them to your mirror!

6. **Take One Step Forward**
   Start small—whether it's taking a moment to breathe and pray in the middle of a hard day, reaching out for help, or trying a new healthy habit. Progress doesn't have to be big to be meaningful. Even the smallest steps can carry you forward when they're rooted in

grace.

Remember, hope isn't about having all the answers—it's about trusting the One who does. Even in the waiting and uncertainty, God is already at work, writing a future filled with purpose and promise. He sees what you cannot, and His plans for you are good.

Chapter 3

What is Love?

A First Love and a First Loss

Sam was my best friend. We met during my sophomore year of high school after I moved back in with my mom and had to change schools, which turned out to be a blessing. Unlike my freshman year, where I felt like an outcast—eating lunch alone at my locker, hiding in the bathroom between classes, and feeling like the poor kid without name-brand clothes—this new school was a breath of fresh air. I still didn't care much about my appearance and had been labeled an "ugly duckling" from an early age, but my best friend was one of the most popular girls in school. Because of her, I found myself with a wide circle of adopted friends and a newfound sense of belonging with the "in" crowd.

Sam was different from my other friends—quiet, kind, and part of what some might call the "loner group." He was a hockey player, so school was more of an afterthought—just something he had to get through to stay on the ice. With little parental supervision, we had jobs, cars, and a lot of independence. He noticed me in a way no one else had—always gentle, encouraging, and present. We spent most of our time outdoors in Alaska, snowboarding in winter, hiking or camping in summer, or simply driving around late into the night chasing the Northern Lights. We dated for a year and a half without a single fight. He made me feel seen, loved, and valued in a way I had never known. Looking back, I believe God placed him in my life to show me what a healthy, loving relationship could look like—something I would need to recognize later when the lines between good and bad became harder to see.

A Tragic Loss

One weekend, Sam and I decided to stay in and watch a movie while our mutual friends went to a party. The next morning, as I was cleaning, my friend John called—clearly distraught. He told me that our friend Cody had been shot at the party in the early morning hours and urged me to get to the hospital immediately. On my way there, Cody passed away.

Still in disbelief, I arrived at the hospital convinced I would find him alive and well. Instead, I walked through the trauma center doors and saw his body covered by a white sheet.

Cody and I had grown up together in the same church community. We weren't best friends, but more like siblings—he was slightly older and always looked out for me. After elementary school, we went down different paths. He had his struggles, and I had mine, though in different circles. But no matter what, Cody remained one of the kindest, most gentle souls I knew. He would've given someone the shirt off his back, even if it meant he'd go without. That kind of selflessness was evident in the turnout at his funeral. The auditorium where we had grown up running through the pew aisles was filled to capacity—standing room only in a space that held up to a thousand people. People of all ages came to honor him.

It was my first real encounter with death, and it shook me to my core. I remember placing my hand on his coffin — saying goodbye yet feeling completely numb. I hadn't cried—not when I heard the news, not on the way to the hospital, and not even at the funeral, surrounded by hundreds of grieving faces. Something in me shifted that week, though I didn't realize it at the time. A quiet unraveling had begun.

I started to drift—slowly, like a fall leaf carried by the breeze. Restless and unsettled, I broke up with Sam a few weeks later by letter. I broke his heart. I used the classic excuse, "It's not you, it's me." The truth? I couldn't face the weight of my emotions—old wounds of loss and abandonment now compounded by a new, jarring grief I had no tools to process.

Cody became just another loss I buried deep, one I refused to acknowledge or feel.

Understanding Codependency

Before sharing the details of the relationships, I found myself in after Sam, I want to introduce you to the nature of codependency. It's a quiet kind of emotional struggle where past trauma makes it hard to know your true worth. On the outside, someone might seem fun, friendly, or easy to get along with—but deep down, they're afraid of being alone. That fear can make them stay in unhealthy or harmful relationships just to avoid feeling abandoned or alone.

Expert Melody Beattie, author of *Codependent No More*, connects codependency to childhood trauma and dysfunctional family environments, showing how early experiences shape these patterns. In romantic relationships, codependency often shows up as excessive caretaking, blurred boundaries, emotional highs and lows, and losing sight of one's own identity.

I'm including this explanation here because these were the exact dynamics I was unknowingly stepping into. Understanding codependency helps explain why I kept returning to relationships that were painful and unhealthy—and why breaking free was such a challenge.

"You don't have to set yourself on fire to keep someone else warm." – Unknown

Logan: The Toxic Relationship

Logan was the quintessential "bad boy." When I was with him, I felt like the only girl in the world, but when I wasn't, I wouldn't hear from him for days—sometimes weeks—because he was busy making other women feel the same way. He was afraid of attachment and thrived on control. I was the perfect target— young, desperate for love, eager to please, and willing to overlook every red flag. My mom and I fought constantly about him. She imposed curfews and rules, which I disregarded entirely. Eventually, she had enough, she recognized I was in trouble and sent me to an outpatient Christian therapy center in Seattle for two weeks. She was hoping being away from him for a period of time would alleviate my need for him in my life. While the therapy was beneficial in some ways, my heart wasn't open to healing at that time. I returned home and immediately moved in with Logan—a mistake of monumental proportions.

Trapped and Isolated

At sixteen, I had no business living with him. I dropped out of school, convinced it held no value for my future. Logan had me exactly where he wanted—isolated, with no car, no job, no school, no social connections. I wasn't even allowed to leave the apartment without his permission. If I left without asking, he would lock me out for hours, claiming it would keep me from doing it again. We fought constantly, because of everything I "did wrong." He came and went as he pleased, cheated on me, and controlled every aspect of my life.

The reality is, many people caught in relationships like this don't fully understand why they stay—or how they got there in the first place. Codependency creates emotional patterns that make individuals more vulnerable to abuse—whether physical, emotional, or both. Emotional abusers are skilled at recognizing these vulnerabilities and exploiting them to maintain control. They manipulate love, self-worth, fear of abandonment, and a desperate need for approval and people-pleasing.

Abusers often test boundaries early on, seeing if their partner will stand up for themselves. They may shower their partner with intense affection or grand promises, creating emotional dependency. Sometimes they present themselves as victims in need of saving—perfectly knowing codependent people thrive on fixing others because they struggle to fix themselves. They create an emotional rollercoaster, alternating between affection and cruelty to keep their partner unstable and craving validation. Over time, abusers cut off social support, deepening the partner's dependence.

I'm sharing this because it describes exactly the relationship I lived in. Understanding these patterns helped me finally see the full extent of what was happening. After years of counseling, I came to terms with how those toxic dynamics shaped my life.

One evening, about a year and a half into the relationship, I was cleaning the apartment and cooking dinner when he came home in a foul mood. We fought like always because I had somehow failed his impossible standards. Through tears, I asked, "Will you ever really, truly love me?"

He looked me in the eyes and said, "You have to earn it."

I was seventeen, standing in the fading sunlight, realizing that if he couldn't love me, no one could. I had nothing— I had cut off all communication to my friends and my family. I had no money, no car and no job. I had hit rock bottom, completely hopeless. But at that moment, I also knew I had to leave. The only person I could think to call was my best friend from high school, Brittany. She picked me up, and I walked out the door— unnoticed, unloved, and discarded.

If you find yourself relating to this story—feeling trapped in a cycle of pain and control—I want you to know there is a way forward. Recognizing these patterns is the first step to breaking free and reclaiming your identity and hope.

"You teach people how to treat you by what you allow, what you stop, and what you reinforce." – Tony Gaskins

Emotional abuse doesn't leave visible scars, but it takes a deep emotional and mental toll. Studies have shown that it can be even more damaging than physical abuse, especially when it comes to long-term effects like depression, anxiety, and PTSD—even in women who didn't experience physical violence at the same time verywellhealth.com. This isn't just theory—it's what I lived through. Years of emotional abuse chipped away at my self-worth and stability, leaving wounds that ran deep and reshaped how I saw myself and my world.

I did not know any of this at the time, that day I knew I just had to get away. I knew I was not in a mental state to continue walking down this path. That day, I saw where the dark road I was on could lead—into depression, maybe even suicide, or a life numbed by alcohol and drugs. And I knew deep down, I didn't want to go down that path. Add this to the list of all the trauma and pain that was piling up but not being dealt with and you could say I continued down the pain rollercoaster.

"Love should not mean losing yourself." – Unknown

A New Chapter

For the next two years, I couch-surfed, partied, and continued a cycle of self-destruction. I worked at different jobs. I would get bored at one and would hop to another one on a whim, convinced the next would be better. I did finish high school thankfully, through mail in correspondence. I numbed my pain with alcohol, drugs, and meaningless relationships. There were sections of time in my memory that I was not sober for many 24-hour periods. I had run out of money and jobs, so I moved back into my mom's house. Then, I met Michael—a sweet, kind, and gentle guy. God was once again offering me a way out, but I was too broken to accept it. I sabotaged our relationship about a year in by cheating on him with my ex, Logan.

Then, life took an unexpected turn. What was supposed to be a routine appointment for birth control at the local Planned Parenthood turned into a moment that would change my life forever. I had planned a night out with my girlfriend, but before heading out for the evening, I stopped in for my appointment. A simple urine test turned into a counselor stepping into the waiting area and calling me back to her office.

I remember the stack of pamphlets fanned out on her desk. "I'm Pregnant, Now What?" sat right on top, followed by "Let's Talk Abortion Options," and underneath it all, buried at the bottom, was "The Benefits of Adoption." My stomach tightened as she informed me that my routine pregnancy test had come up positive.

"Do you have any questions?" she asked gently.

I sat in that tiny office, gripping the armrests of the green plastic chair, feeling like the walls were closing in. My mind was blank. I was in shock. "No questions," I muttered. She handed me the stack of pamphlets, and I walked out in a daze. On the way home, I stopped at a drugstore and bought two more pregnancy tests. I took them as soon as I arrived home. Both were positive.

Looking back on that day, I realize I didn't go through a rollercoaster of emotions like some might expect. I had been numb for so long, drowning in alcohol, bad relationships, and self-destruction, that it was just another moment of, "Well, here we are." But I do remember one thing clearly—abortion and adoption were not options for me. I found out I was pregnant. It wasn't the result of a perfect relationship or ideal circumstances, but rather, it became the catalyst for change. This baby was not a consequence—it was a gift, a reason to fight for a better future. For the first time in years, I saw a glimmer of hope, a chance to break the cycle and build something new, not just for myself, but for the life growing inside me. Pregnancy gave me the motivation I never had before. It was no longer just about me. And that made all the difference.

By then, my days of couch surfing and staying with friends had come to an end. I had moved back in with my mom to get back on my feet after leaving Logan. The most terrifying part wasn't the thought of raising a baby alone—it was telling her.

Breaking the News

The next day, I went home and told my stepdad, Steve. He was kind, loving, and more importantly, the buffer between my mother and me. When I blurted it out, he stood up, walked to the window, took a deep breath, and said, "I'm going to take your mom on a drive. She can't kill me if I'm driving, and she can't kill you until we get home."

He was right to be cautious and adding humor in the mix was just a normal occurrence in how we all handled the tension in the household. When she found out, her reaction was immediate and harsh. She didn't hesitate for a moment before declaring that I would give the baby up for adoption, convinced it was the only way to ensure the baby or I had a successful future. Her words were sharp, filled with certainty that it was the best solution.

But I wasn't convinced. I was resolute in my decision to keep my baby.

Her face grew cold, and with a finality that left no room for negotiation, she told me to pack my bags and leave.

At the time, it felt like my world had fallen apart. I was devastated and unsure of how to move forward. But looking back years later, I understood that her decision, though painful in the moment, was the best thing she could have done for me.

It forced me to stand on my own, to take responsibility, and to grow up. For the first time, I was forced to think about someone else—my baby—and that shift in perspective would start to shape the course of the rest of my life.

A Glimmer of Hope

With nowhere else to go, I moved in with my good friend's parents. They had an extra room and took me in without hesitation. His father owned a car mechanic shop, and he found an old 1980s Blazer in a junkyard, he fixed it up, installed seatbelts, and gave it to me. It was dependable and safe—perfect for when the baby arrived. Another glimmer of God's provision.

I got on WIC and welfare to ensure I had healthy food during my pregnancy. I worked two minimum-wage jobs to save money, determined to stand on my own. The couple I lived with were incredibly kind — almost too kind. They treated me like the daughter they never had, and my unborn baby like the grandchild they had always wanted. But at the time, I wasn't ready for that kind of love. It overwhelmed me. I felt unworthy of it. I moved out on good terms and rented a room from one of my sister's friends.

A New Beginning

The rest of my pregnancy passed without any major issues. My ex—the baby's father—wanted nothing to do with me or the child, even after the paternity test confirmed he was the dad. Over time, my mom softened toward me. Though I never moved back in with her, she was there for the birth and offered some financial support.

Then, he arrived—my sweet, special baby boy. I named him Austin, a name that symbolizes strength, courage, and leadership. From the moment I held him, I knew he was a miracle. We were a team.

Austin was an easy baby, sleeping through the night and showing the sweetest personality. He was my little buddy, always by my side when I wasn't working. Everyone who met him instantly fell in love.

Despite her initial hesitation, my mom grew to adore him. She helped care for Austin while I juggled multiple jobs, often keeping him overnight. During this time, I also started reconnecting with old friends—some who had gone on to college, others moving forward in life. For the first time, I allowed myself to envision a future beyond mere survival.

God had been quietly planting seeds of hope all along. I couldn't yet see the full picture, but the path to healing had begun.

Takeaway: Finding Hope Even When Life Doesn't Look Like You Imagined

Life rarely follows the neat, predictable path we envision. Sometimes, it takes turns we didn't expect, bringing uncertainty, hardship, and moments where hope feels distant or fragile. It's okay to admit that things don't always make sense or feel fair. In fact, accepting this reality is often the first step toward finding true hope.

Hope doesn't require perfect circumstances or a clear roadmap. It's not about pretending everything is fine or rushing to have all the answers. Instead, hope can be a quiet, steady presence that holds space for the messy, difficult, and unknown parts of life. It's the small light that flickers in the shadows, inviting you to keep moving forward even when the way isn't clear.

This chapter of my story reminds me—and I hope reminds you—that hope can emerge even in the darkest moments. It's found in unexpected places, in new beginnings that don't look like what we planned, and in the courage to keep going despite uncertainty.

The Bible speaks to this beautifully in Psalm 46:1-2: *"God is our refuge and strength, an ever-present help in trouble. Therefore, we will not fear..."* Even when life feels overwhelming, we don't have to face it alone. There is a refuge—a safe place—where hope can take root and grow.

Sometimes, hope means learning to be okay with the detours and delays, trusting that there is purpose beyond what we see. It's about giving yourself grace to feel lost, broken, or uncertain, knowing that these seasons don't define your whole story.

If you're walking through a dark season, know that it's okay to not have it all figured out. Hope isn't about the destination alone—it's about the willingness to keep stepping forward, even when the path is hidden.

Your life may not look like you imagined right now—and that's okay. Hope is not a promise that everything will be easy or perfect, but a confidence that there is good ahead, even when you can't see it yet.

Remember Romans 12:12: *"Be joyful in hope, patient in affliction, faithful in prayer."* Let this be your guide as you navigate your journey—hold on to hope, even when the road feels uncertain, and trust that healing and light are coming.

Chapter 4

A Dangerous Path

A New Beginning Turned Nightmare

When my son was only a few months old, I found myself drawn into another relationship, fueled by a desperate desire for stability and protection. I had always craved a strong presence to guard me from life's chaos—and he seemed to offer just that. His uniform, his demeanor, and his charm felt like a safe harbor after the emotional storm I'd been living in. I ignored the red flags and, just six months later, married him. That choice would become one of the most devastating decisions of my life.

On the surface, it looked like we were building a happy home. But behind closed doors, everything shifted. What I had mistaken for strength revealed itself as control, and what I thought was kindness dissolved into dominance. He used his position and size to manipulate and intimidate. In public, he played the part well—kind, attentive, even fatherly. But in private, I lived under the constant weight of fear, walking on eggshells in my own home.

Thankfully, my son spent most of his time at my mother's house or with his father's family. Somehow, he was shielded from what I was enduring. And for that, I was endlessly grateful.

A Weekend in the Middle of Nowhere

Just a few months into the marriage, I was told we were going to spend a weekend away at a remote military post. He was a military police officer so he had told me he had to take his turn patrolling the remote location and that family could go. He said the buildings were vacant but functional—electricity, water, everything we'd need. It was miles from the nearest town, and the drive was long, rainy, and silent. When we arrived, I realized just how truly isolated we were.

I passed the time watching movies and reading while he "worked." But on our final night there, something strange happened. I was sitting on the couch, half-distracted by the TV, when I saw a reflection in the window—his silhouette standing behind me. I startled and turned quickly, heart pounding. He brushed it off, but something about the moment felt off—haunting, even.

That memory faded into the recesses of my mind until nearly two decades later, when I was in counseling. Through a dream,

God brought it all rushing back. In that dream, I saw an angel standing over me that night, arms stretched wide. I didn't know the full extent of what could have happened, but I knew without a doubt that I had been spared. Even when I didn't ask for help—even when I'd made damaging decisions—God still protected me.

> *"The LORD will keep you from all harm—He will watch over your life. The LORD will watch over your coming and going both now and forevermore."*
> —Psalm 121:7–8

The Beginning of the End

Nine months in, everything exploded. What began as a simple request by me to take out the trash turned into a violent outburst. Things were thrown. Words cut like knives. In a moment of ultimate fear, I grabbed the keys on the counter as I bolted out into the rain, desperate to get away, jumped into our truck, and locked the doors. But even then, escape wasn't simple. He leapt into the bed of the truck as I pulled away, ripped the back window from the setting and climbed inside through the rear window opening while I was still driving.

I made it just short of the base police station, threw the car in park and ran as fast as I could to the front door. I arrived visibly shaking. I gave my statement to a female officer who, after a few questions, and not many pen strokes on her yellow steno pad, dismissed the incident as a typical domestic argument. He was sent to the barracks to sleep it off and I was sent home alone to rest.

Escaping the Nightmare

The next morning, I received a call from his commanding officer. The officer asked me if I wanted him to return home—implying that not allowing it would ruin his career. I was 19, terrified, and now feeling pressured by a superior to make a decision I was never qualified to make. But somewhere deep inside, I knew. If I said yes, I may not survive.

With help from friends and family, I finally left. One of my friends—also a young mom—listened as I shared the full weight of what I had endured. She didn't hesitate. She made a few calls and soon connected me with someone who had a small room available to rent. It wasn't much, but it was safe—and it was mine.

With what little strength I had left, I packed up my belongings. Some went into storage in my mom's garage. The rest I brought with me to the new place. My dad, seeing how desperate I was to start over, stepped in and paid for me to attend nail school. That act of generosity was more than financial—it was a vote of confidence that I could rebuild.

Shortly after that, my friend helped me get a job at a local day spa. It was owned by two incredible women who created a warm, supportive environment. One of them had just had a baby and had hired a full-time nanny. When she heard about my situation, she offered to let Austin stay with the nanny while I worked—at no cost to me. It was a miracle I didn't expect, and I remember standing in the break room one afternoon, tears in my eyes, realizing that God was already piecing together what I thought was permanently shattered.

The Stalking Begins

At first, it was just texts.

Then calls.

Then names of places I had just been.

It was clear—he was watching me. Somehow, some way, he knew where I was and who I was with. The messages became increasingly unsettling, not just in frequency but in tone. One moment he was remorseful, professing his love and regret. Next, he was accusing and manipulative. His presence loomed even in places where I thought I was safe. I recognized how quickly things could escalate, so I made sure Austin stayed with his dad or my mom throughout most of this time.

Friends urged me to file a restraining order. But I hesitated. Not because I didn't believe he was dangerous—I did. But I feared provoking him further. I was terrified that taking legal action would make him snap, that it would throw gasoline on already smoldering coals.

Then one afternoon, while I was out with friends, he appeared. Out of nowhere. He confronted us, visibly angry. Voices rose. I stood between him and my friends, my body instinctively moving to de-escalate the moment. Eventually, he left—but the encounter rattled me to my core.

Later that night, the rain came. I sat with my friends at the apartment where I was renting a room, trying to find some sense of calm when my phone rang. His voice was on the other end.

"I just want to talk," he said. "Please. I love you. I can't live without you."

"I don't think that's a good idea," I replied, keeping my voice calm but firm.

"Come outside," he said, his voice low and chilling. "I'm by your car."

Panic set in. He had found me—again. My safe place was no longer safe. The walls closed in. I could feel the familiar tightness in my chest, the heat of anxiety crawling up my neck.

My friends, God bless them, didn't hesitate. They urged me to call the police immediately, and this time, I did.

When the officers arrived, I told them everything—about the messages, the earlier confrontation, the phone call, how he knew where I lived despite my efforts to hide.

They listened. Then one of the officers asked, "Do you have a restraining order on file?"

I told him I planned to file one the next morning, based on everything that had happened that day.

He looked at me—sympathetically, but with resolve.

"I'm really sorry," he said quietly, "but I have to place you under arrest."

What?

I could barely process the words. My knees buckled beneath me.

He explained that earlier that day—right after the public incident—my ex had gone to the police first. He had filed a statement claiming I was the aggressor. And because he had beaten me to it—because his report was on file first—I was now being treated as the threat.

The cold metal of the handcuffs wrapped around my wrists as tears streamed down my face. The humiliation, the fear and the shame—it was all too much. I was the victim, and yet I was the one being taken away in a patrol car.

I spent two days in jail. Two long days where I questioned everything—my decisions, my life, my ability to protect myself and my child.

But even in the coldest, darkest corners of that cell, God was still there.

He sent rescue in the form of my sister's boyfriend, a lawyer who stepped in and went to work immediately. When we stood before the judge, the truth broke through. My case was dismissed on the spot.

But what we discovered next was chilling.

When my lawyer requested the records from my previous police report on base—the one from the night I fled to the base station, the one where I gave a statement—the report was gone. Vanished. No record. No proof. It was as if it had never happened.

Someone had erased it. Buried it. Left me defenseless.

Still, the judge already saw the full picture. He granted me a long-term restraining order and apologized for what I had been through. My lawyer filed for divorce immediately.

And just days after being served, it was told to me that he had attempted suicide in his barracks, and he was hospitalized in a therapy center. We had to secure legal permission to proceed with the divorce while he was under medical care. I had to sit across from him in a small hospital room with my attorney and the doctor in the room to sign the divorce paperwork.

I left that day legally free—papers signed, marriage dissolved—but emotionally, I was still deeply entangled. The chaos had ended, but the silence that followed was just as loud. I didn't know how to process what I had been through, and I didn't have the tools to begin healing. I had stepped out of one storm, only to realize I was still standing in the wreckage. Freedom on paper didn't mean peace in my heart. In many ways, I felt even more lost—numb, detached, and unsure of who I was or how to move forward.

By all logic, I should have been a shattered version of myself. And in many ways, I was. But something deeper held me together—a spiritual tether I couldn't sever. Even though I had been detached from my own emotions for years—unable to feel joy, sadness, or even anger—I still believed there was more. I didn't know how or when, but I knew God wasn't done with my story.

I had lived the same painful year on repeat, numb to life. But eventually, I realized *this* had to end. I was no longer willing to live stuck in survival mode. The cycle had to break.

If You're in a Dangerous Relationship—There Is a Way Out

If something inside you feels off—if you're constantly walking on eggshells, afraid of how someone might react, or being isolated from people who care about you—please know this: you're not overreacting, and you're not alone. Abuse doesn't always start with bruises. It can be emotional, verbal, financial, spiritual—or a mix of all of these.

Here are a few quiet first steps you can take:

- Document what's happening. Keep a private journal or notes (saved in a safe place) about incidents, threats, or controlling behavior.

- Tell someone you trust. A friend, a family member, a mentor—someone who will believe you and help you stay grounded in truth.

- Create a safety plan. Know where you would go in an emergency. Keep essentials like copies of IDs, money, and keys in an easy-to-grab spot.

- Reach out for help. You can call or text the National Domestic Violence Hotline (800-799-7233 or text "START" to 88788). They will never pressure you— they just listen and guide.

It takes courage to admit you need help, and even more to take action. But your safety, sanity, and soul are worth it. You are not weak for leaving. You are brave for choosing to live.

You were not made to live in fear.
There is life beyond survival.
There is hope beyond this season.

Finding Hope on the Wrong Path

Sometimes, we choose the wrong road. Not just the wrong turn—but the entire road. We ignore the warning signs. We justify the red flags. We convince ourselves that love will heal what's broken, or that loyalty will make someone change. We cling to hope in all the wrong places, sometimes confusing self-sacrifice for virtue and endurance for faith. But the truth is, not every path leads to life—and not every person we invite in is safe.

And yet... even there, in the dead-end places of regret, *God finds us.*

Like the father in the story of the Prodigal Son (Luke 15:11–32), He watches from a distance—not to shame us, but to run toward us the moment we turn His way. That son didn't return home clean or composed—he came covered in the mess of his choices. And yet the father didn't hesitate. He embraced him, clothed him, celebrated him. God doesn't need perfection to begin restoration. He simply needs our willingness to come home.

His protection shows up in the midst of chaos. His mercy guards us even when we don't recognize it. His love covers us when shame wants to bury us. Psalm 34:18 reminds us that *"The Lord is close to the brokenhearted and saves those who are crushed in spirit."*

Even when we walk down dangerous paths, hope is not lost. If you've made choices you regret... if you've stayed too long... if you've silenced your intuition or believed too little—you are not too far gone. Your past may explain your pain, but it doesn't define your future. God's healing is still available.

Because with Him, no road disqualifies you, and no chapter is too messy to be rewritten.

Hope begins the moment you let Him walk the rest of the way with you.

Chapter 5

A Foundation for Healing

Romans 7:19 (NIV) – "For I do not do the good I want to do, but the evil I do not want to do—this I keep on doing."

Brokenness and the Weight of Past Choices

Broken people make broken decisions. The trauma of my past and the brokenness I carried in my heart became the compass guiding many of my choices. Like shattered glass, each decision added another fracture—another broken piece of a life I didn't fully understand. For years, I lived in the aftermath of choices that mirrored a pain I couldn't admit to—the kind that leaves a permanent mark on the soul and distorts everything it touches.

Only a few months after my first marriage ended, I met Matthew. He was different from the others I had dated—calm, collected, reliable. Traits I desperately craved after the chaos of my first marriage. Matthew was an interpreter, fluent in multiple languages, with a grounding military career. He seemed like everything I thought I needed. But there was one glaring issue: he was an atheist and didn't want children. I was a Christian—though not practicing—and I already had a child. He tolerated Austin and was pleasant, but you could tell he was relieved when Austin left to spend time at his dad's home or with my mom.

At the time, those differences didn't resonate as deal-breakers for me. My emotions had become a solid, unreachable block. I was numb. So numb, in fact, that when Matthew proposed just weeks after we met, I said "yes" without hesitation. Deep down, I knew something wasn't right, but I had no capacity to grasp the weight of that decision.

We married in a courthouse. Though I cared for him, I didn't love him. Love had become foreign to me. I clung to the idea of safety and stability, convincing myself that real love wasn't meant for someone like me. I felt disqualified by my past mistakes—too broken for anything truly good. So I settled. Our life was functional, but never full. We lived in a small downtown apartment, coasting through the motions of married life without real connection.

When Matthew received deployment orders for a six-month tour, I didn't feel the usual heartbreak that many militaries spouses experience. There was no anticipation of absence, no emotional preparation, no grieving of the "lasts." For most military families, those final weeks before deployment become sacred. You begin to cherish the smallest things—the last dinner out, the last grocery run, the last movie night on the couch. Even mundane moments take on weight because they become the final memories to hold on to while you wait and hope for a safe return.

But for me, none of that happened.

There was no lump in my throat as the days dwindled down, no intentional effort to savor what was slipping away. I didn't cry when he left. I didn't feel much of anything. I said goodbye like I'd see him in a few weeks and carried on with my life as though nothing had changed. The truth was, I had been emotionally disconnected from Matthew from the beginning. So when he boarded the plane, it didn't feel like a loss—it felt like permission. Permission to slip back into my old life, my old patterns, my old crowd. I didn't even pause to reflect. I simply fell back into the arms of distraction—nights out, partying, and pretending I was still single, still unbound.

I was emotionally adrift, untethered from everything that should've grounded me—marriage, commitment, integrity. And when Matthew found out, when the stories reached him halfway across the world, it must have cut deeper than I'll ever fully understand. From thousands of miles away, in a desert not his own, he made the decision that should have been obvious long before: he asked for a divorce.

He didn't yell. He didn't beg. He simply let go—maybe because he realized he had never truly had my heart in the first place. And I didn't fight it. I didn't cry or plead. I accepted it with the same numb detachment I had lived in for years. The unraveling of our marriage wasn't sudden. It was slow and silent, like a thread that had been fraying for months, maybe even from day one.

The morning after he called and asked for the divorce, I walked into the courthouse and filed the paperwork. It felt like paying a parking ticket—another mundane errand. I moved my belongings into storage and crashed with a friend. I didn't cry. I didn't grieve. I didn't feel guilt or remorse. I felt nothing.

Matthew flew home halfway through his deployment to try and talk it out. But I was already gone—emotionally shut down. As I walked away from him in a hotel parking lot after meeting with him and hearing his pleas to try to work it out, I felt a strange mix of apathy and relief. I had closed a door that never should've been opened. A few days later, our marriage was annulled, I was 22 years old.

The Redemptive Power of Unexpected Love

"Sometimes, when things are falling apart, they may actually be falling into place." – Unknown

I had given up on love. After so much heartbreak and betrayal, redemption felt out of reach. Honestly, I'm not sure I even knew what real love was. But God, in His quiet way, was orchestrating something I couldn't have foreseen.

Daniyel entered my life when I wasn't looking. A mutual friend, Juan, mentioned him, but I wasn't interested. I was still reeling from two divorces, trying to rediscover who I was apart from any relationship. Daniyel, too, had just come out of a painful marriage. We both agreed to meet for a drink, thinking nothing of it. But the moment I saw him; something stirred in me.

He had a mysterious presence—handsome, grounded, with a quiet confidence that intrigued me. He didn't need fixing. He wasn't seeking validation. That was both comforting and terrifying.

At that time, I was still deep in unhealthy behaviors—drinking, partying, numbing. He took my number with a casual promise to call, and over the weeks we kept in touch. Our connection deepened. His unpredictable military schedule created space between us, but oddly, it allowed us to grow.

Then came a wave of loss in his family: his grandfather, grandmother, father, and stepmother—all gone within a year. He traveled back home multiple times, and we stayed in touch through each family goodbye. God's hand was quietly working. The distance protected us—giving our fragile bond a chance to strengthen without pressure.

Eventually, Daniyel met my son, Austin. They clicked instantly. Austin, then three, was spending half his time with me and half with his dad. He had a nasally chipmunk voice, chubby cheeks, and a belly laugh that lit up every room. Everyone who met him loved him and seeing Daniyel with Austin began to soften something hard in me. I wasn't healed yet, but I began to feel hope.

Marriage as a Catalyst for Change

After about a year of dating, we made the decision to move in together. Looking back, it felt more like a decision rooted in convenience than one grounded in readiness or intentionality. We enjoyed each other's company, we laughed often, and life, for me, felt lighter together than it had in years—but we were both still carrying our own emotional baggage.

For me, the unresolved anger I had buried for years hadn't gone away—it had just been waiting for a safe enough space to resurface. And that's exactly what our home became: a place where I could finally begin to feel. Instead of dealing with those feelings, I often redirected them—through irritability, through control, through outbursts that even I couldn't explain. I didn't know how to communicate what I needed because I hadn't yet learned to identify it myself.

Daniyel, on the other hand, brought his own silent struggles into our home. His emotional distance wasn't about coldness or lack of care; it was survival. His trauma had taught him to tuck his emotions away, to keep them under control, and to never let anyone get too close to the places that hurt. He didn't shut down out of malice—he did it out of protection. And I didn't know how to respond to that. I wasn't used to someone who didn't need rescuing, who didn't fall apart and ask me to fix it. So instead of leaning in, I avoided pushing. I kept my questions to myself, tiptoed around hard conversations, and settled into an unspoken agreement: I won't press if you won't pull away further.

We drank, and that never helped. Alcohol always distorts reality. It intensifies pain, turns confusion into chaos, and fuels the lies we already believe about ourselves. After my outbursts, panic attacks would often follow—racing heart, shallow breathing, chest tightness that made it feel like I couldn't catch my breath. I didn't know what was happening at the time. I thought I was broken beyond repair. But I would later learn that those symptoms were the body's way of finally feeling safe enough to release what had been stored for years. My trauma wasn't new; it was just finally rising to the surface.

About a year into living together, Daniyel received orders to deploy to Iraq for six months. We had discussed marriage a few times, but he always found a way to brush it aside. There were a few reasons. He was uneasy about the financial debt I had accumulated—it felt like instability to him; a red flag tied to his deep need for security. And then there was the lingering pain from his previous marriage. During his last deployment, his ex-wife had been unfaithful, a betrayal that ultimately ended their relationship. That wound hadn't fully healed.

Though it was never directly stated, I came to understand that part of him believed if I could remain faithful through this deployment, maybe then he could trust me enough to take the next step. In his mind, it became a silent test—proof that I was different, that our relationship was different. And while I understood where his fears came from, we would both come to recognize later in our marriage that this was an unhealthy place to begin. Building trust through silent tests and unspoken expectations laid a shaky foundation. But even in that mess, God was present. He was quietly working, preparing us both for a deeper healing we didn't yet know we needed.

When Daniyel deployed, something in me shifted. I knew I didn't want to repeat the same patterns this time. This relationship felt different—it was steady, safe, and for the first time in a long while, I could see the possibility of a healthier future. I began making changes. I started taking Austin back to church, distancing myself from the party scene, and surrounding myself with people and places that aligned with the person I wanted to become.

About a month before Daniyel was scheduled to return home, I brought up marriage again. My time in church and in reflection had stirred a conviction in me about the way we were living—sharing a life without the covering of a true commitment. I explained what was on my heart, not as an ultimatum but as a sincere desire to honor the growth we were both experiencing. He didn't give an answer right away, but a few days later, he called and agreed. If we were going to move forward, truly and fully, then marriage was the next step.

He returned on October 1, and just six days later, on October 7, we were married in a small, intimate ceremony at the lake, officiated by my stepdad, Steve. It was simple and sincere, just close family and quiet joy. That December, we held a larger Christmas wedding with friends and extended family—a celebration of not just our union, but of how far we had both come.

Healing and the Slow Unraveling of the Past

Marriage didn't fix everything. It added new challenges. I was still battling anger and anxiety. Daniyel still numbed his pain with alcohol. But we were learning, slowly—how to be better people, partners, parents.

We bought a house. I started a bookkeeping business and worked part-time at my mom's fine dining restaurant. We continued attending church regularly together. A year later, we had a fiery little girl named Grace Taylor.

Her birth was a turning point. Daniyel's love for Grace was immediate and full. He bathed her, fed her, rocked her when she was sick, and read to her. They were two peas in a pod. He poured his heart into being the father he had never had. I loved having a little baby around to love on, and I found so much joy in watching her discover the world around her. From day one, Grace had an independent and stubborn streak. You never had to wonder how she felt—she made sure you knew, one way or another. We always said she was destined to be a world changer with that strong personality. But she also brought so many hilarious moments. She loved to make us laugh and thrived as the center of attention in our home. Austin also embraced being a big brother. Some of my favorite moments were when Grace would do something silly just to make Austin laugh, and I'd hear both of their belly laughs echoing through the house.

It felt good to be building something worth fighting for.

But healing isn't linear. The anger, fear, and anxiety still surfaced sometimes. Yet God continued weaving our lives into something beautiful. And like any masterpiece, it takes time—full of knots, tangled threads, and hidden stitches.

> *Lamentations 3:22–23*
> *"Because of the LORD's great love we are not consumed, for his compassions never fail. They are new every morning; great is your faithfulness."*

You may still feel the sting of what you've walked through. Maybe the nights are quieter, but the thoughts are louder. Maybe you've left the situation, but parts of it still live in your body—your reactions, your fears, your doubts, your shame. That's okay. Healing doesn't happen overnight. It isn't a straight path or an overnight revelation.

Some days, you'll feel progress. Others, like you're starting over or maybe even like you have regressed. But if you're moving—even slowly—you're not stuck. Every step matters. Every time you choose truth over shame, calm over chaos, rest over self-blame or repentance over isolation—you're healing.

The middle place between pain and restoration is sacred ground. God meets us here.

A Whisper in the Wilderness

One of the most powerful reminders of God's kindness in the middle is the story of Elijah in 1 Kings 19. After a great victory, Elijah was overwhelmed and afraid. He ran into the wilderness, collapsed under a broom tree, and asked God to end his life. But God didn't rebuke him. Instead, He gave him rest. He sent an angel to feed him, let him sleep, and gently whispered, "The journey is too much for you."

Later, God met Elijah—not in the wind, or the fire, or the earthquake—but in a gentle whisper. He didn't just rescue Elijah; He restored him.

So, take a breath. Don't rush. You're allowed to grow slowly. You're allowed to grieve and still believe good things are ahead. Even here, in the in-between, hope is rising. Like Elijah, you don't have to be perfect. You just have to keep showing up—because the same God who whispered in the wilderness walks with you now.

Chapter 6

The Role of Community in Healing

"Two are better than one, because they have a good return for their labor: If either of them falls down, one can help the other up." — *Ecclesiastes 4:9-10 (NIV)*

Four years into our marriage, Daniyel and I were living what looked like the typical all-American life. We had sold our home in town and moved onto base in Alaska, preparing for the inevitable set of new military orders that signified a move to a new town. By then, Daniyel had already extended his stay twice, completing two full four-year terms, and we knew our time in Alaska was coming to an end.

Outwardly, everything seemed steady. Daniyel continued working at the fire department on base, and I focused on growing my bookkeeping business from home while caring for our daughter Grace. Austin was thriving in school, and our days were filled with the familiar rhythms of military family life. We went to church regularly, maintained superficial friendships, and attended the usual community events. But under the surface, our marriage was lacking intentionality. We were coasting. Our conversations hovered around logistics. We moved through the motions without passion or purpose, waiting for the next day to arrive, rarely reflecting on how we were actually doing.

Then the orders came: we were headed to Keesler Air Force Base in Biloxi, Mississippi. I had never heard of Biloxi, but when I looked it up, the first image I saw was a lighthouse overlooking the beach. Without missing a beat, I turned to Daniyel and asked, "So, how fast can we pack?" Living by the beach had always been a dream of mine, and this felt like the fresh start we both needed.

However, one significant challenge remained: joint custody of Austin. His biological father, now divorced and still entrenched in a party lifestyle, had been resistant to discussions that centered around letting us take Austin with us when we moved. Although he had fallen behind on child support, he clung to the 50/50 custody arrangement as a way to avoid financial responsibility. We offered a bold proposal—if he agreed to relinquish parental rights and allow Daniyel to adopt Austin, we would waive rights to all future child support.

At first, he agreed. We filed the appropriate paperwork and prepared for the adoption hearing, scheduled just days before our move. But two days before the court date, he called to say he had changed his mind and had filed paperwork to withdraw his previous approval. That night, I didn't sleep. I wrestled with fear and uncertainty. How was I going to move across the country and leave my child behind? How would the logistics even work? Would I be forced to choose between staying with my son or continuing life with my husband and second baby?

Praying brought a little peace, but not enough to quiet my racing thoughts or bring sleep. The next morning, tired and weary, we walked into the courthouse unsure of what the day would bring. When the clerk called the case, we saw that the defendant's side of the courtroom was empty. The judge asked where they were, and the clerk explained that no continuance had been requested. Austin's biological father had simply not shown up.

The judge was visibly frustrated that, after submitting a formal withdrawal, Austin's father hadn't considered it important enough to attend the hearing. After confirming with Daniyel, the seriousness of what he was agreeing to—accepting the full rights and responsibilities of a child who was not biologically his—the judge approved the adoption.

Austin was officially a Blankenship.

It was one of the most emotional and powerful moments of our family's journey. For years, Austin had been forced into a situation that wasn't healthy or safe. I had spent countless evenings dropping him off with tears in his eyes and praying he would be protected until he came back home. That chapter finally closed, and our family felt whole.

If you are a parent working through a custody battle right now, I want to pause and speak directly to you. I know how heavy and heartbreaking it can be to send your child into an environment you know is not healthy. I know what it feels like to stand helplessly at the edge, watching someone who is supposed to protect and love your child make choices that seem anything but loving.

Sometimes, hurt people make selfish decisions—ones that benefit themselves but not the child. And sometimes, as the parent trying to do the right thing, you have to keep showing up, even when the legal system doesn't feel like it's working in your favor. You may have to send your child into a place that goes against everything in you. It doesn't make you weak. It makes you brave. It makes you faithful.

So, I implore you: don't give up. Fight legally. File the paperwork. Advocate. Use Google if you have to in order to fill out the court paperwork yourself without an attorney. Do what it takes, even if you have to do it scared. The nights and days may be long and heavy, but there is something being built in the waiting. There is growth happening in the unseen places—in you, and even in your child.

Don't give up hope that the other parent can change. Don't give up hope that the court system can one day see the truth. Most of all, don't give up hope that God is present and powerful, even when you cannot physically be there to protect your child. He sees what you can't. He guards in ways you can't. His arms are long enough to reach them, even when yours are not.

Just don't give up.

As we prepared to leave Alaska, I felt a strange mix of grief and excitement. I was saying goodbye to everything I had ever known, but I also sensed that something new was ahead. I entrusted the Alaska branch of my business to a business partner and prepared to plant new roots on the Gulf Coast. We took our time driving down as a family from Seattle to Mississippi, stopping to enjoy the country along the way. When we finally arrived, the beach was quiet and crisp, and it felt like the first real breath I had taken in years.

We did all the things military families do in a new place—found coffee, housing, schools, a church, a hairdresser, and a new rhythm. At first, we attended a church but struggled to connect beyond the Sunday services. About a year in, we started feeling led to look elsewhere. One of my employees invited me to try her small church. It had about seventy members, mostly military and local families who had services but also shared meals, played games, and prayed together.

It felt like home.

The sense of community was unlike anything I'd experienced since childhood. People did life together, not just worship on Sundays. Daniyel, who hadn't grown up in church, was surprised by the closeness. We were both drawn in. We grew spiritually and emotionally. Our marriage began to deepen. But as is often the case, growth stirred up old wounds.

One Sunday, about a year after we started attending, the pastor preached a message on the difference between conviction and condemnation. The Holy Spirit stirred something deep within me. I had a secret. Actually, I had several.

My emotional outbursts during disagreements had continued, often triggered by deep financial anxiety. Growing up, I had never been taught how to handle money. Instead, I learned to use spending as a coping mechanism. Bad day? Buy a new outfit. Feeling empty? Open a store credit card. It became a habit—a way to soothe myself that only buried me deeper in shame and debt.

Despite Daniyel's early hesitation to marry me because of my financial past, I had not truly changed those patterns. I was managing our family's finances, but behind the scenes, the debt was mounting. At the time of that sermon, we were $50,000 in the hole and Daniyel had no idea. The weight of the lie was suffocating me.

I felt the Lord nudging me to confess. That afternoon, I sat Daniyel down and told him everything. His face went pale. He didn't yell, but he was visibly and understandably angry. Disappointed. Hurt. He grabbed his keys and left.

I was sure it was over. The shame was overwhelming. But this time, I wasn't alone. I had a community. I called Lacy, the pastor's wife and a dear friend. She listened, prayed, and gently told me that her husband Jeremy was already on the phone with Daniyel.

Later that night, Daniyel came home. He wasn't ready to forgive, but he wasn't walking away either. He said we needed a plan. Over the next few weeks, we sat with Jeremy and Lacy and created a strict accountability system. Zero-based budgeting, no personal spending without cash, weekly check-ins. Any dollar over and above what we normally brought in between our jobs was going to debt until it was gone! It was hard. Humbling. But I welcomed it.

Check out some tips at the end of this chapter that we discovered while paying off debt.

A few months into our financial recovery plan, I had managed to save $40 of my personal allowance—a tiny sum by most standards, but it had taken intention and restraint to get there.

One stressful afternoon, I found myself wandering through Target, mindlessly picking up items I didn't need but emotionally justified. It had been a rough day, and my old habit of self-soothing through spending was trying to claw its way back in.

But halfway down an aisle, I stopped in my tracks. My hand hovered over my purse, and I remembered the envelope that held those hard-earned $40. Sixty days of self-discipline were tucked in that envelope. I looked at the items in my cart, then back at the envelope, and I knew in my heart—none of it was worth it. I didn't need any of it. Not for comfort, not for validation, not for relief.

So I placed every single item back on the shelf and walked out of the store empty-handed.

Now, walking out of Target without buying a thing is a feat for any woman, but for me, that day marked a breakthrough. It wasn't just about the money. It was about the power it no longer held over me. Something shifted in my spirit. The emotional grip money had on me—its control over my choices, my moods, my sense of security—was broken at that moment.

And I truly believe that was the release I needed. That was the moment God opened the door for new freedom—not just financially, but emotionally and spiritually. It was no longer about lack or guilt or chasing something to feel better. It became about stewardship, trust, and walking in peace.

It was small, but it was holy.

With diligence, prayer, and community support, we paid off all $50,000 in twenty-six months with no change in our regular job earnings. We also never stopped tithing throughout this entire time. That was something we knew was a catalyst for the rapid debt payoff. When we started doing things God's way, blessings also started to come. Insurance refunds we were not expecting, gifts we were not anticipating. Because we had a plan for every dollar we knew exactly where to put it when it came in and it was targeted. The more obedient we were with the plan and the accountability the faster the debt was paid off.

In the weeks and months that followed, I came to understand even more deeply just how essential community was in that season of our lives. What began with a financial breakthrough began to spill over into emotional healing, much of which was nurtured by the people God placed around me.

Lacy, in particular, became an anchor. Her friendship softened parts of my heart that had been hardened for years. She parented her children with grace and freedom, and she extended that same grace to me. She didn't judge or shame. She didn't lecture. She simply showed up—again and again—with a gentle presence that reminded me I was safe and seen. Through her love and example, I began to realize what genuine, unconditional friendship looked like, and it started to rewrite the way I related to myself and others.

Proverbs 17:17 says, "A friend loves at all times, and a brother is born for a time of adversity." We lived that truth. Without Lacy and Jeremy, I don't know if our marriage would have survived. Without our church family, we would have carried the burden of that debt alone. But God never designed us to walk through valleys without others.

Sometimes healing doesn't come through instant deliverance but through the long, faithful walk of accountability, friendship, and truth-telling. Like Ruth and Naomi walking together through grief and scarcity toward redemption, sometimes God uses the loyalty of others to guide us toward restoration. We had those kinds of people in our lives, and through this process, we learned how to be those people for others.

Healing thrives in community. Hope flourishes when it's shared.

Not every storm is stilled immediately, but every storm is survivable when you aren't standing in it alone.

Strategic Debt Payoff Tips: Real Steps That Brought Us Freedom

1. Give Every Dollar a Job.
   Create a zero-based budget where every single dollar is assigned a purpose before it hits your account. This

includes income from side gigs, bonuses, refunds, and any unexpected blessings. If it comes in, it goes on a mission.

2. <u>Have a Personal "No Questions Asked" Allowance.</u>
Both spouses should have a small, agreed-upon monthly amount to spend however they wish. Ours was $20 per month. It gave us freedom within boundaries, which helped reduce stress and resentment during tight seasons. If you want a fancy dinner or you want to get your nails done then you have to SAVE for it.

3. <u>Use a Real-Time Budgeting App.</u>
Use an app that syncs your accounts so you can both see transactions in real time. It keeps you accountable and helps you course-correct quickly if you are overspending.

4. <u>Use Cash for Problem Categories.</u>
Groceries, eating out, and household items are all cash-only. Pull out the budgeted amount each month and once the cash is gone, that category is closed. This alone changed how we spent and what we prioritized. It's inconvenient but so is your debt!

5. <u>Make a Rule for "Extra" Money.</u>
Any money outside your regular paycheck—gifts, bonuses, tax returns—go straight to debt. Always. No exceptions until every balance is zero. It isn't glamorous, but it worked. You don't need a new couch

or a spa day. Pay off that debt and then you can buy as many couches as you want for cash!

6. <u>Have Weekly Budget Check-Ins.</u>
Sit down together once a week—even for 15 minutes—to go over the budget, check progress, and talk through upcoming expenses. It keeps you both on the same page emotionally and financially. NOTE: these may start out with fights the first few times but STICK to the plan and keep meeting. It WILL get easier.

7. <u>Start with the Smallest Debt First.</u>
The snowball method worked for us. Tackle the smallest balance first for a quick win, then roll that payment into the next one. Momentum builds motivation.

8. <u>Cut Unnecessary Subscriptions and Expenses.</u>
Pause streaming services, gym memberships, and anything else that isn't essential. Every dollar saved becomes a soldier fighting your debt.

9. <u>Celebrate Milestones (Creatively).</u>
When you pay off a credit card or hit a milestone, celebrate in budget-friendly ways—picnics, homemade desserts, or even just a high-five and a praise report to your friends.

10. <u>Remember the Why.</u>

Keep a sticky note on the cash envelopes with the word *freedom* and a Bible verse to remind yourself why you are making the sacrifice. Keeping your eyes on the purpose can give you endurance in the process.

Chapter 7

Confronting the Reality of Childhood Pain

"He heals the brokenhearted and binds up their wounds." — *Psalm 147:3 (NIV)*

Having a healthy community around you—filled with supportive friends and mentors who encourage you to grow—is crucial when you begin digging into past pain. I was a high-functioning woman on the outside: a business owner, mother, wife, leader, and volunteer. But beneath that surface lived buried pain that would erupt in the form of anxiety attacks, insomnia, outbursts of rage, and an overwhelming sense of dread. Life wasn't broken, but it wasn't full either. I had checked the boxes—marriage, children, career, church—but deep inside, I felt there had to be more.

God slowly started to widen my lens. I began to notice that people who lived full, peace filled lives were not free from hardship—they just responded differently. The ones who seemed to thrive were those who pressed in when life got hard. They didn't retreat. They sought more of God, leaned into community, and fought for growth. I realized that kind of life required intentionality.

Unpacking Memories

One day while unpacking during a move while living in Mississippi, I found a book I'd received during an intensive counseling retreat I attended at sixteen. It was called *The Seven Keys to Spiritual Renewal*. It wasn't a NY Times best seller, but it stirred something in me. The word "hope" came up in my spirit again. As I thought back to that experience, I remembered the conversations and some small breakthroughs that happened during therapy then. Maybe, I thought, it was time to go back.

I checked with our insurance and scheduled a counseling session. The first meeting was brief and ended with a prescription for anxiety and sleep medication. I was labeled a stressed military spouse, and I left feeling unheard. I tried again with another counselor in the same office. She was quirky and disarming. We connected, and she invited me to write out a life timeline—a record of what I considered the major events of my life, both good and bad.

That exercise wrecked me. I had blocked out more than I realized. As I listed those events, memories and emotions began to rise to the surface. Though we began discussing them in our sessions, I wasn't ready. I quit a few sessions in. The soil had been disturbed, but I wasn't prepared to keep digging.

We have to recognize when we're ready to face the hard stuff. That doesn't mean waiting until we're no longer afraid. If you wait for fear to leave, healing will never come. You have to be brave in the face of fear. You have to lean on community for encouragement. And you have to put one foot in front of the other—even if they're small steps. Sometimes though, you also need to pause and process. That's okay too.

About a year later, Daniyel and I reached an impasse due to my recurring anger. Our pastors referred us to a counselor. We attended a few sessions together, and afterward, I saw the counselor on my own for the next year.

He didn't rush to medicate. He gently asked questions and listened. Slowly, we began unpacking the trauma of my childhood and teen years—moments I had long buried. With grace, David helped me see that my anxiety, panic, and anger weren't random. They were symptoms. They were my soul's way of alerting me to wounds left untreated.

Understanding Trauma

"The cure for pain is in the pain." — Rumi

Trauma shows up in many forms. For some, it's acute trauma—a single, shattering moment. For others, like me, it's chronic or complex trauma: prolonged exposure to pain that becomes part of how you see the world and yourself.

Chronic trauma slowly distorts your inner compass and complex trauma—often rooted in childhood—forms when escape isn't an option. It impacts everything: how you regulate emotions, how you relate to others, and how you view your worth.

Anger, anxiety, panic—these are the signals. For me, they were red flags waving in the face of unprocessed pain. My body had been sounding the alarm for years, but I didn't know how to fix it. And truthfully, I had never really thought about myself as someone who had experienced "trauma."

To me, that was a victim word. I didn't want to categorize myself that way. I was too busy walking around as an independent woman who had it all together—or so I told myself. I wore strength like armor. But underneath it, pain simmered.

Healing rarely follows a straight path. It also doesn't follow a tidy timeline. But it begins with acknowledgment.

David helped me speak the truth: "That was painful. That was trauma."

Just naming the hurt opened the first door to healing. It didn't solve everything overnight, but it began the process of chiseling away at my hardened heart. I wasn't alone. I had friends. I had faith. Most importantly, I had God gently leading me forward.

Taking Responsibility

Acknowledging the pain was one thing—but taking responsibility was another. Some wounds, like my parents' divorce or the emotional needs that went unmet in certain relationships, were never mine to carry. They weren't my fault. But healing required more than just recognizing where I'd been hurt. I had to face the truth: if I wanted real freedom, I couldn't stay stuck in blame or victimhood. I had to accept reality for what it was—and own the fact that I had made choices along the way that caused pain, both to myself and to others. Growth began when I stopped excusing my actions, stopped blaming my parents for the pain of my childhood, and started surrendering it all—my hurt, my pride, and my need to be right—so I could finally begin to heal.

I knew right from wrong. I had grown up with a foundation in faith. Yet I had rebelled. I dated men my parents warned me about. I numbed my emotions with alcohol and toxic relationships. I ignored red flags. I rejected accountability and counsel. And those choices had consequences.

Accepting that truth was hard. Pride said I didn't need help. Shame said I was beyond redemption. But grace whispered, "There's more for you," and I believe God is whispering that to you today.

God had already begun weaving healing into my story—through a loving husband, a new home, faithful friends, and safe spiritual leaders. The healing had started long before I realized it. And I was finally ready to participate in it.

What is God shining His light on in your heart or past today?

Maybe it's a memory you've tried to forget, a pattern you can't seem to break, or an emotion you've buried for years. Maybe, just maybe, this is the moment He's inviting you to begin.

I pray you'll take that step—yes, even in fear—toward healing and wholeness. Don't wait until it's easy or you feel "ready." Trust that He goes before you, walks beside you, and carries you when needed. One brave step is all it takes to begin.

"He who began a good work in you will carry it on to completion until the day of Christ Jesus." — Philippians 1:6 (NIV)

Journey to Freedom

I had participated in the *Freedom* group before at our church, but this time, I felt called to lead it. The curriculum was designed to guide believers into deeper inner healing—addressing the pain in our mind, body, and spirit through God's Word.

During one quiet time, I felt the Lord gently nudge me to begin weaning off the anxiety and depression medication I had relied on for over fifteen years. I had tried before without success, but this time felt different. It wasn't a decision driven by fear or rebellion—it was born from a deep desire for healing and wholeness.

Let me be clear: I believe medication is a gift and sometimes necessary for certain seasons of life. I would never suggest anyone stop taking it without the guidance and care of a trusted medical professional. That said, I knew God was inviting me into a new level of freedom, and with my doctor's support, I began the process for myself.

I wanted to trust God—and myself. I wanted to feel deeply and process emotion, not suppress it. I was finally ready to move forward. I prayed, I journaled, and I meditated on Scriptures like Jeremiah 29:11: "'For I know the plans I have for you,' declares the Lord, 'plans to prosper you and not to harm you, plans to give you hope and a future.'" And Philippians 4:13: "I can do all things through Christ who strengthens me."

I began to believe those words again.

Nine weeks later, I was completely off the medication. Not out of denial—but out of peace. I had learned to treat my emotions as signals, not commands. My thoughts no longer controlled me.

Since that breakthrough, I've remained free from anxiety medication. Through counseling, support, and growing closer in my relationship with God, I gained tools to identify my triggers and respond in healthier ways. This freedom didn't come overnight, but it did come—and it continues to grow. I believe you can experience this freedom too!

Forgiveness and Letting Go

It was also in that group where I began to forgive—not just others, but myself. That part was harder than I expected. I had carried so much shame from my past—shame from choices I'd made, things I'd tolerated, and the lies I had believed about my worth. For so long, I had looked at myself through a distorted lens, one clouded by pain, shame, and the voices of people who didn't see my value. I couldn't recognize the person God created me to be because I was so focused on who I had been and what I had done.

One night, I wrote in my journal: "God, help me see myself the way You see me." It wasn't just a prayer—it was a desperate cry for a new vision, a new identity. I was tired of feeling disqualified by my past. I wanted to believe that I was more than the mistakes I had made. And in His grace, He answered.

He didn't speak in thunder or write it in the sky, but little by little, He began to shift the way I saw myself. Through Scripture, through community, through moments of quiet surrender, He began to whisper truth into the parts of me that had long been buried in lies. I started to see glimpses of the woman He always saw—whole, loved, chosen, and redeemed. That simple prayer became a turning point in my healing. Because when you begin to see yourself the way God sees you, everything changes.

I forgave the men who had hurt me. Not because what they did was okay, but because they were broken, too. They didn't have the knowledge or tools to love me the way I needed to be loved. I wasn't excusing the sin, but I was releasing the grip it had on my heart.

It was in that group I first heard the statement: Unforgiveness is like drinking poison and expecting the other person to die.

Forgiveness was no longer about them—it was about freedom for me. It did not happen overnight but once I made the choice the feelings followed.

Ecclesiastes 3:1 says, "To everything there is a season, and a time for every activity under heaven." Healing is no different. I couldn't do it all at once. Like a crock pot—not an Insta-Pot—God simmered the pain slowly, tenderly, over time.

He knew when I was ready. And when He brought things up, I trusted He had already placed the people and tools around me to handle it.

Family Counseling and Inner Healing

A few years later, Daniyel and I faced parenting challenges with Grace. We were frustrated. Uncertain. Honestly, we were questioning our ability to parent well because things were so emotionally chaotic for all of us. We didn't learn the right parenting tools when growing up, so we sought a family counselor. Enter Sarah.

She taught us about "family plans"—pre-agreed expectations and consequences that both kids and parents commit to ahead of time. The idea was to have a plan in place *before* the crazy cycle started—the one where a child disobeys because they're tired and hungry, and the parent yells because they're exhausted and it's the 40th time they've said the same thing. By the end, everyone's upset, and doors are slamming around the house. But this approach changed everything. Discipline no longer triggered chaos. We had structure. We had peace. We had an agreement we had all signed and instead of yelling or slamming doors, we were able to all take accountability for our behavior and any consequences because of the written plan we had all agreed on.

But counseling did more than help our family. It opened another door for my own healing. During a personal session one afternoon, Sarah had me close my eyes and imagine myself as a child. She asked me what I saw. As I sat in that counseling room chair, I saw a seven-year-old girl, with long blonde hair, curled up, crying on the steps of her childhood home.

This memory was new. Until then, I had only remembered happy childhood moments—snow forts with my brothers, gardening with Mom and our family vacations.

But now, sadness surfaced. I remembered our family dog dying. Feeling rejected by my sister. And the day I found out my dad was gone.

These were wounds I hadn't yet faced. But now, I had the tools to confront them. I didn't numb the pain. I talked about it—with Sarah, my pastors, and my friends. And talking brought healing. I even was able to talk to my sister and start to repair the broken relationship we had had for so many years. Today we are great friends and have an amazing relationship built on trust and communication.

John 8:32 says, "Then you will know the truth, and the truth will set you free." And Revelation reminds us that we overcome by the word of our testimony.

Speaking the truth—bringing it from darkness into light—was where freedom lived. None of it would have been possible without God, faithful friends, and my willingness to finally face it.

Final Thoughts

"The journey of healing starts with a single step, no matter how small." — Lao Tzu

Healing isn't a finish line—it's a lifelong invitation. And the beautiful thing is God walks with us the whole way.

He sends the right people. He opens the right doors. And when the time is right, He brings light to even the darkest corners of our hearts.

We just have to be willing to say yes. What small step in your healing journey can you say yes to today?

Chapter 8

Just a Wink Down the Yellow Brick Road...

Moving Forward, Together

As my story moved ahead, so did the lives of my family. My brothers both found love, married, and began building families of their own. My oldest brother had settled in rural Michigan with his wife's family, and my mother—tired of enduring the punishing winters of Alaska—finally persuaded her husband, Steve, to start over in Michigan.

They bought a beautiful home just down the street from my brother. It was tucked away behind a grove of trees, perched on a hill like something out of a storybook. A red barn stood proudly to one side, a green tractor always parked just so, purple, blue and white hydrangeas lined the porch rails that wrapped around the home with rocking chairs that creaked to the rhythm of sunrise and sunset.

Michigan still had winter, but it didn't bite the same way Alaska did. My mom settled in full-time and nurtured the land, while Steve gradually reduced his hours at the nonprofit he had led for decades in Alaska. He would travel back and forth between Alaska and Michigan every few months in what he called "semi-retirement." The home they created became a kind of sanctuary, a space where peace resided in the quiet details. The top floor held my mom's sewing studio and Steve's beloved library, a place filled with old books, framed poetry, and a quiet stillness that whispered of decades of service and thought.

The heart of the home—the middle floor—was open and warm, centered around a massive stone fireplace that seemed to breathe comfort. The kitchen was always alive with scent and sizzle, as if some culinary artist lived among them. At the back of the house, a wall of glass invited the woods to come inside. Chipmunks darted past in the mornings. Occasionally, a deer would pause just long enough to remind you of God's handiwork. It was stillness in motion.

My relationship with my mom, once strained, had grown steady by this point. We talked often—sometimes about serious things, sometimes just sharing recipes or the joys of whatever was blooming in our gardens. I tried to visit at least once every year or two, sometimes with my husband Daniyel and our kids, Austin and Grace, in tow. They loved the farm life—splitting logs, dumping compost from the golf cart, and running wild with their cousins under open skies. These moments became the stuff of family folklore: s'mores by the fire, homemade ice cream and card games that lasted until midnight. The home welcomed everyone, and in doing so, became a place we would all carry in our hearts.

But as life teaches us again and again: nothing stays the same.

A Life-Altering Phone Call

I was deeply involved in my church, serving as a worship leader and singing most weekends while helping to mentor and lead our team. This role required weeknight rehearsals and participation in all of our weekend services. Worship and music are as essential to me as air and breath. They are woven into my DNA, a gift from God, a calling embedded in my heart. Both my parents had led worship, as had my grandparents. It's not an obligation or tradition—it's a piece of who I am-a worshipper.

That Sunday morning began like any other. We had just wrapped up rehearsal, and I was walking toward the green room backstage to pray before service. My phone rang. It was my mom.

Something in her voice made time stop.

> "Hope, I called Daniyel—I didn't know what else
> to do...
> Steve is dead."

Those words pierced through the noise of my world like glass shattering in slow motion. I stopped walking. I couldn't breathe. Couldn't make sense of what I had just heard.

She explained in hurried words: Steve hadn't shown up for church. She rushed home and found the shower running, the door locked, no answer. Firefighters broke down the door. Steve was gone.

Cardiovascular failure. Just like that.

In that green room, I collapsed into Daniyel's arms as tears streamed down my face. The man who had quietly shaped my teenage years through wisdom, humor, and unwavering support was gone in a moment.

Processing the Loss

I rushed to Michigan. I needed to be with my mother, needed to handle the flood of paperwork that comes with death—but more than that, I needed to see it to believe it. I needed to sit in his chair, touch his books, hear the silence he left behind.

In those early days, I moved like someone underwater. Funeral arrangements, financial documents, legal calls, well-meaning condolences—all came crashing in, and none of it filled the space he left. I remember sitting in his chair looking out over the green grass to the sun setting just behind the barn. How could someone so alive, so thoughtful, so needed... just disappear?

Steve wasn't loud or flashy. But he was a steady light—wise, kind, funny in an understated way. We didn't talk every day, but when we did, our conversations mattered. He challenged me intellectually and spiritually, often sending me quotes, articles, or book recommendations. He cared deeply about the world and spent his entire career empowering individuals with disabilities to live fully and independently. He was sought after by universities in Austria and across Europe, eager to learn from his expertise. Even as he neared retirement, he contemplated pursuing his doctorate overseas.

And now, he was gone.

The Weight of Grief

> "There is no pain so great as the memory of joy in present grief." —Larry Stansbury

They say grief is a funny thing. I disagree. To me, grief is pain— deep, relentless pain. It's isolating, consuming, and cruel. I understand now why people withdraw, why they struggle to re-engage with life after loss. Grief strips away our illusion of control, leaving us vulnerable and lost. The five stages—denial, anger, bargaining, depression, and acceptance—sound neat on paper, but in real life, they're messy, overlapping, and circular.

Some days, I'd feel a flicker of hope—enough to reach for my phone, ready to call him—only to remember he wouldn't be on the other end. And just like that, the weight of loss came crashing back. Holidays reopened wounds I thought had started to heal. And yet, over time, I began to understand something important: grief doesn't go away. It weaves itself into the fabric of who you are. It becomes a quiet companion—not to overwhelm you, but to remind you of the love that once filled the space now left behind.

Grief is not a problem to be solved. It is a presence to be felt—and to be carried, not alone, but alongside love, faith, and memory.

Steve had been many things to many people—mentor, friend, leader, teacher. His death reminded me that everyone who touches our lives leaves a mark, often in ways we don't fully recognize until they're gone. And so, I made a choice. I could disappear into the dark corner of my sorrow, or I could carry his light forward.

Every time I choose kindness, I'm choosing Steve. Every time I laugh with my kids or encourage a friend, I'm honoring him. His influence didn't end with his last breath. It lives on—in me, and in everyone else he poured into.

"Until We Meet Again, Down the Yellow Brick Road..."

Those words ended the last letter Steve ever wrote me. Three months before he passed, he mailed me a bound collection of his poems and musings. One of them, *THAWTS*, had been written shortly after I gave birth to Austin. It still hangs in my bedroom.

I read it often—especially when his absence feels heavier than usual. I hope you enjoy this poem.

THAWTS – By Stephen P. Lesko

If all the Frogs were Princes, and all of the Ladies Queens, If all of the World was a Castle, and all of the Guards, Jellybeans....

There might be no today nor tomorrow, Let all of the Past roll away, With silver soft sewn in the moonbeams, and rainbows at break of day...

Then all the boys who would live there, And all of the girls, dressed in gold, Might freeze in that magical moment, Of storybook legends told....

There children would speak in sweet visions, Perhaps it would be you or me, Enchanted in innocent beauty, and forge all the Royal Decrees...

"Let all of this life's dreary hatred, rise like an army to war, and march on with fear, discontentment, to be banished from here, evermore..."

"Let poverty ne'er be remembered, and hunger-a word long forgot, with want, and with need, desperation, to never return to this spot...."

"Let Wind-songs, and Carols, and Poems flow through the twilight's deep mist, and every new babe fore the nite-tide, be tucked in its cradle, soft kissed..."

"Let gentleness carve us the roadways, and love be the street lamps at night, let stars be the wonders we wish on, and wishes go soaring like kites..."

Growing old- would only be- a memory..... You and I- would be nothing but dreams... If all the Frogs were Princes.... and all of the Ladies, Queens....

His writing was whimsical and wise, playful and profound. In his own way, he gave me one final gift: permission to dream, to hope, to live lightly in a world that often feels so heavy.

Grief That Grows Us

What grief are you carrying today?

It's a sacred question. Grief hides in plain sight—at the grocery store, behind a smile, under the surface of a prayer. It waits for quiet moments, for anniversaries, for unexpected reminders. It teaches lessons we didn't ask to learn, about time, about love, about the fragility of it all.

But what if we honored our grief instead of resenting it?

What if we saw it as proof of deep love?

Grief reminds us to live with intention. To savor our mornings. To call our people. To say the words. And if we let it, grief can also teach us how to be more like the ones we lost. More generous. More open-hearted. More present.

Allowed its sacred work, grief strips away the trivial and reveals the eternal. It turns our eyes heavenward, drawing us toward the heart of God. Grief is not evidence of His absence; often it is the place we find Him most tenderly present. He built us for community—to weep, hope, and heal together.

It won't always feel like this. The pain dulls. The memories sweeten. The ache gives way to gratitude. And in that space, you may find yourself being transformed—not because grief destroyed you, but because God met you in it.

You were created with a purpose no one else can fulfill. Perhaps, in the center of your sorrow, lies a seed of hope someone else desperately needs. Let your healing become a gift. In God's hands, grief can blossom into grace.

When Jesus Weeps With Us

John 11 tells of Lazarus and his sisters, Mary and Martha. They sent word to Jesus, believing He could heal, yet Jesus delayed. Lazarus died. Their faith and pain collided:

> "Lord, if You had been here, my brother would not have died. But even now I know that God will give You whatever You ask." —John 11:21-22

When Jesus saw Mary weeping, *"Jesus wept"* (John 11:35)—the Bible's shortest verse, yet one of its most profound. The Son of God paused to feel human sorrow. He didn't rush them. He joined them. He dignified their tears before He raised Lazarus.

God never rushes us through pain.

If you are mourning today, know this: Jesus sees, Jesus cares, Jesus weeps with you. And just as He called Lazarus to rise, He is calling something inside you to rise as well. Maybe not today, maybe not tomorrow—but hope waits on the horizon.

Grief changes us. But so does love.

And maybe, just maybe, part of your healing will become the beginning of someone else's hope.

Life remains. Purpose remains. So, we walk—together—just a wink farther down the yellow brick road.

Chapter 9

Healing from the Inside Out

There's something about motherhood that holds a mirror to your soul. Having kids has taught me more about myself than any book, course, or counseling session ever could—if I'm being honest. Children are funny that way. They reveal the best and worst parts of you, not through confrontation, but simply by existing, watching, and reflecting you back to yourself in a thousand tiny ways.

From the very beginning, I have loved my children with all my heart. I cherish them deeply. But I wasn't the overly affectionate, snuggly type of mom. I didn't bake cookies every week or plan Pinterest-perfect birthday parties. I am the Venmo for class parties and buy lunch at school mom. What I also am, is intentional. I see my role as a sacred one—called by God to raise humans who can think, live, love, and lead with purpose. I want to raise responsible adults who can not only contribute to the world but reflect God's love while doing it.

But early on, I also made lots of mistakes.

When I started my business, I poured myself into it. I was juggling marriage, motherhood, entrepreneurship, and personal growth all at once—and often, I dropped the ball on what mattered most. I worked long hours and often weekends. I prided myself on providing for my kids physically: clothes, a safe home, healthy food, clean beds. But emotionally? I was running on empty. I struggled with things like affection and verbal affirmation. I didn't say "I love you" often. "I'm proud of you" didn't come naturally. I was a mom who could handle structure and survival, but I wasn't yet a mom who could sit in emotions, who could lean into presence over productivity.

I wasn't patient. I wasn't soft. I wasn't aware.

At church I am known as the mom who will do anything - I'd clean toilets, stack chairs, be a greeter at the front door, work in admin, I'll even run sound for service—anything but serve in the children's department. I love kids... just not in that way. I didn't feel called to their world. It felt messy, chaotic, emotional and uncomfortable but I am so appreciative of those who are gifted in this and that is truly a blessing!

Then everything changed—slowly, subtly, but significantly— when my son Austin grew old enough to join the church's youth group. He got involved with the worship team and started playing piano. He had never been one to be super passionate about any one thing in particular or really with anything. He is super smart and hysterical. He is responsible and has always followed all the rules. He is a very logical and linear thinker. When he started playing piano on the worship team, I saw passion start to develop in him. He blossomed in that space. It was like watching a flower open in real time.

And God, with His gentle sense of humor, pulled me in behind him.

Serving in youth ministry was never part of my plan. I had zero desire to hang out with hormonal, smelly, loud teenagers. Many of them came from broken homes, with absentee parents, rough backgrounds, and visible walls around their hearts.

But I showed up. At first, it was just to support my son. But God had another agenda entirely.

I began to get to know the students. I started to listen to their stories, observe them in moments of vulnerability and joy, pain and hope. And something in me started to shift. Their stories touched places in my own heart that I didn't even realize were still tender. My assumptions about them—their rudeness, their chaos—began to fall away. And in their place, compassion began to grow. My heart softened.

One memory stands out in particular. Every year, the youth group hosts a turkey scavenger hunt around Thanksgiving. We split up into teams, each led by an adult, and roam around town completing hilarious challenges. Some of them included taking selfies in store bathrooms, making strangers laugh, videoing silly interactions with cashiers. That year, I led a group of five girls— some I knew, others I didn't.

One of them was Ella.

Ella was like a beam of sunshine with feet. She radiated joy, playfulness, and energy. She had no shame, would try anything, and brought laughter wherever she went. But underneath that bright exterior, I soon discovered, was a deep well of strength and resilience. Ella came from a broken home. She didn't grow up in church, aside from the once-in-a-while visit on Christmas or Easter. She had been invited by a friend and fell in love with the community our church offered. Over the months, we spent more time together. I listened to her story and her questions. Her transparency taught me more about empathy than any leadership training ever had.

She was relentless in her pursuit of joy. It was contagious.

But even more impactful was how her openness helped me see myself differently as a mother and a parental role in my kids' lives. Watching how she processed conflict, asked for guidance, and leaned into wisdom made me reflect on how I spoke to my own children. Her willingness to be vulnerable gave me permission to be more present. More verbal. More affectionate. I started telling my kids I loved them. I told them I was proud of them. I became more intentional with my actions and my words.

Ella helped me become a better mom without ever knowing it.

Today, she's married to my son Austin, and I can honestly say she is one of the greatest gifts to our family. She brings light into every room. And she played a part in healing parts of me I didn't even know were broken.

Consequently, Ella wasn't the only relationship God used during this season of transformation.

Around the same time, I began growing closer with our campus pastors, Jeremy and Lacy. They are the kind of people who just *get* others—kind, patient, funny, and deeply wise. They became a safe space for me. We'd talk for hours—about life, ministry and parenting. We often shared meals, dreams, frustrations, and fears.

Over time, they transitioned from being new friends to spiritual mentors, and eventually, like family. And unknowingly, they became vessels God used to re-parent my heart.

Dr. Henry Cloud, in his book *Changes That Heal*, says, "God can use our current relationships to provide nurturing we didn't receive as children, the mentoring we missed as school-aged kids, or the companionship we needed as teenagers." I remember reading that line and feeling like someone had just turned on a light inside of me.

God was using Lacy and Jeremy to do just that. Not in any official capacity, but simply through presence, consistency, and love. They filled gaps that had long gone unmet in my life. They spoke into places that had been silent for too long.

One summer, I attended a silent sabbatical retreat through our church business group. Fifteen women, three days, no phones, no distractions—and twenty-four full hours of complete silence. As an extrovert, the thought of that was absolutely terrifying. But it turned out to be one of the most healing experiences of my life.

We stayed on a quiet, secluded property with old trails and small knolls—remnants of a closed golf course. On one hill stood a tiny white chapel with stained-glass windows and wooden pews. It felt sacred. Like stepping into another time. That morning, I walked into the chapel and settled onto a pew, taking in the scent of cedar and years of emptiness. I sat there in silence, breathing in the stillness, and letting God speak without interruption.

And He did.

That day, through prayer, journaling and reflection, God began to show me the threads of healing He had been weaving in my life over the past few years. He gave me insight into my past, clarity about my future, and a deep appreciation for the people He had placed along the way. I wept but it was not from sadness. The tears came as I began to realize the pain from my past, that held me for so long, was being miraculously redeemed.

It was the beginning of a deeper self-awareness than I'd ever known.

For the first time, I could see my journey clearly—how meeting Ella softened my mother-heart, how time with Lacy healed my daughter-heart, and how God was using these relationships to make me whole again. He had removed the hardened parts of my heart and replaced those empty spaces with love and grace through others.

This journey also led me to examine my relationship with my own mother. It wasn't all bad. My parents provided a home. We had food, safety, and structure. They raised us in church. My mom taught me how to cook. She taught me how to take care of a household, and I know I gained the gift of hospitality from her. She was the best at hosting people and making them feel welcome and at home. We had family vacations and spent time camping in the Alaskan wilderness. They did their best.

Like all of us, they had pain. Unprocessed pain will often leak into other areas of our life. For my parents that pain leaked into our relationship.

Growing up, emotional expression wasn't encouraged. Back then mental health was taboo in society. Vulnerability felt dangerous and disagreements happened behind closed doors. Kids were meant to be seen, not heard.

I've learned that we all parent with the tools we have at the time. In the history of parenting there has never been a parent fully equipped to raise a child. Everyone is missing something from their toolbox. However, this doesn't mean that our parents didn't love us. It just meant that they also needed a little healing and some help too.

When we don't heal, our unprocessed trauma can spill into our children's lives in the form of control, fear, withdrawal, or perfectionism. But, when we do the work and let God in, generational patterns can be broken permanently making a way for new cycles of wholeness.

That's what healing from the inside out is really about.

We often understand physical healing—we get a cut, we clean it, bandage it, let it scab and scar. We respect the process.

But emotional wounds? We tend to ignore those. We hide them, downplay them, and often intentionally bury them in the crevasses of our heart. We "move on" while still bleeding inside. But untreated emotional wounds don't disappear. They fester. Harden. Scar in ways that deform how we love, lead, and live.

I've learned that healing is not weakness. It's wisdom.

> Proverbs 2:6:
> "For the Lord gives wisdom; from His mouth comes knowledge and understanding."

It's choosing to face the pain rather than run from it. It's letting God into places we'd rather forget. It's inviting trusted people to walk with us in the dark until we find light again. It's learning to accept the unearned, undeserved, but always available Grace of God.

God is the ultimate healer. We see many stories in scripture of Him healing physically but also emotionally and spiritually. He binds up the brokenhearted (Psalm 147:3). He's gentle with our pain and patient with our process. He's not in a rush. He sits with us in the silence and holds us in the storm.

Healing doesn't mean forgetting. It doesn't mean we pretend the pain never happened. It means the pain no longer controls us. It means the scar becomes a sign of God's faithfulness rather than a reminder of our brokenness.

So, if you are carrying deep regret, betrayal, childhood pain or disappointment I want you to know that healing is possible. Healing is part of the Christians inheritance. It's not a detour from your destiny. It's part of it.

Emotional and spiritual healing doesn't happen by accident—it's intentional. Just like we schedule doctor appointments when we're sick or clear our schedules to rest when we're physically exhausted, we must carve out space to tend to the soul. Healing is a process, not a destination. And that process often begins with one small courageous step.

Here are a few practical ways we can begin—or continue—the journey of healing from the inside out:

1. Seek Wise, Faith-Based Counseling

Healing often requires guidance. Professional counseling can be one of the most powerful tools in our journey especially when that counselor shares your faith and foundational values. A Christian counselor, in particular, can help integrate biblical wisdom with psychological insight. They provide a safe, confidential space to unravel the layers of past trauma, current patterns, or mental blocks without judgment. Sometimes, just having an unbiased person to listen and allow us to freely say what we think and feel can be the beginning of clarity and hope.

Don't be afraid to ask for help. Healing isn't weakness—it's wisdom.

2. Surround Yourself with Supportive Community

God created us for connection. When we're hurting, isolation often feels easier but it's in a community where real restoration begins. Find friends who will sit with you in your grief, who will laugh with you when laughter returns, and who will remind you of who you are when you've forgotten. You don't need a crowd—you need a core. Even one or two trusted friends can make all the difference.

Healing multiplies in safe, loving environments.

3. Step Away from the Noise

Take a retreat, a weekend away, or even a long afternoon by yourself—whatever you can manage away from your normal routine. The key is to intentionally not pack it full of errands, sightseeing, or tasks. Let it be quiet. Let it be slow. Reflect. Rest. Pray. Listen. Often, God speaks most clearly when the rest of the world is turned down low.

Stillness is not wasted time. It is sacred space.

4. Journal Your Journey

Grab a notebook or open a blank document and start writing. Not for anyone else's eyes. Just yours—and God's. Pour out your real thoughts, fears, questions, and dreams. Don't worry about grammar or eloquence. The healing comes from honesty, so write how you truly feel. Writing allows you to name what you're experiencing. By naming it, you begin to tame it. Sometimes, the clarity we seek comes after we spill the words we didn't know were buried inside.

Write even if you never share it. Your soul needs a witness.

5. Say It Out Loud Over Coffee

Sometimes, we need to speak our pain to loosen its grip. Grab coffee with a trusted friend or mentor and allow yourself the gift of being heard. You don't have to spill everything. Just a piece. A part. As much as you're comfortable with. Speaking it aloud can lighten the load, bring clarity, and open the door to empathy and encouragement.

You don't have to walk through this alone. Even Jesus had close friends in His hardest moments.

6. Feed Your Mind with Insight and Encouragement

Reading books or listening to audiobooks about what you're experiencing can be both validating and empowering. Whether it's a memoir from someone who's been through something similar, or a book that offers biblical wisdom and psychological tools. These resources can serve as lifelines when you feel adrift. They can help you put language to what you feel and hope where you feel stuck.

Sometimes someone else's words will unlock your own.

7. Learn How You're Wired

Self-awareness is the foundation of healing. Take some personality assessments to better understand how you process information, handle stress, or receive love. Tools like the Enneagram, Meyers-Briggs, DISC, or Five Love Languages can offer practical insight into how you're designed—and how your design influences your decisions, relationships, and reactions. The more you understand yourself, the more you can extend grace, make aligned choices, and break free from shame or confusion.

Understanding how you're wired can be the beginning of walking in wholeness.

8. Practice Self-Compassion

You can't rush healing. You can't expect sunshine every day while walking through a storm. Some days you'll feel like you've made progress, and the next day may bring tears again. That's okay. Give yourself grace. Go slow. Be kind to yourself. Hard things take time, and time takes trust.

Your pace doesn't disqualify your progress.

9. Write Your Eulogy—Through Your Kids' Eyes

This one is not for the faint of heart—but it's powerful. Take some quiet time and write your eulogy as if it's being read by your children. What would you want them to say about you? What kind of person do you hope they remember? What do you want them to carry forward because of how you lived? This exercise is sobering—but it also offers clarity. It gives you a blueprint for the kind of legacy you want to build and the steps you may need to take to get there.

> *Let purpose shape your healing. Let vision shape your choices.*

Let Him into the quiet places. Let Him stitch your heart back together with love, truth, and grace. Let Him surround you with people who will speak life when you can't find the words yourself.

Just like your body, your heart was never meant to stay broken.

> "God can heal a broken heart, but He has to have all the pieces." – Unknown

Chapter 10

Grace Over Perfection

If grades had been given for social skills when I was in school, I would've been a straight-A student. Honor roll. National Honor Society. Maybe even valedictorian—at least in the category of connecting with people. I was the kid whose mom got called because she talked too much in class. Making friends was never the problem. Unfortunately, school wasn't about connection—it was about comprehension, and that's where I struggled. I can count the number of A's I received throughout my entire school experience on one hand.

I attended a small, local Christian school from kindergarten through sixth grade. By second grade, it became clear that I learned differently. At the time, there weren't widespread labels or conversations around learning disabilities, and I never heard the word "dyslexia." I truly thought my learning experience was normal. Several times a week, a few of us would head to a separate room to work on phonics and memorization in the afternoons. It felt like a small club. I had no idea it was the special needs class. We had an amazing teacher who encouraged us, met us where we were, and never made us feel less than. Looking back, I now recognize I had dyslexia—and those sessions gave me foundational tools I still rely on today. Isn't it funny how, as children, we are often unaware of the foundational things being built in us? We simply show up, follow directions, do our best—and all the while, God is laying the groundwork for something greater. What feels ordinary in the moment can later reveal itself as purposeful preparation.

High school was a shock. In ninth grade, I transferred to a large public school where I knew no one and carried my learning challenges into an environment that had little support for students like me. I failed both Spanish and French and nearly failed English. I think my teacher graded my tests on a very generous curve just to help me pass. Halfway through 11th grade, I dropped out. I thought, *Why keep struggling when I could just start working and making money?*

Eventually, I completed a year and a half of coursework through a state correspondence program in just four months. It was writing-based—no tests, no memorization—which is probably the only reason I finished. My diploma came in the mail. No graduation. No celebration. Just an envelope.

Over the next 19 years, I tried college off and on, mostly online. I love learning, but reading and retaining information has always been difficult. What I did love was working. I excelled in jobs that used my creativity, people skills, and work ethic. I was often promoted quickly and eventually started my own bookkeeping business, which continues to thrive today almost 20 years later.

Still, I've had plenty of awkward moments in professional settings: "Where did you go to college?" "What's your degree in?" I used to mumble a response, ashamed. Living in the South, where alma maters are worn like badges of honor and college football loyalty can be a deeper bond than shared DNA, not having a university name to drop felt isolating. Around here, people don't just go to college—they *belong* to it. Their graduation year, Greek affiliation, and game day rituals are all part of their identity. So when I answered, "I didn't go to college," I often felt like I was handing them a reason to doubt me. It was as if my credibility expired before the conversation even began. I'd shrink back, smile politely, and quietly hope the conversation would move on. But here's what I've come to realize: I don't need to apologize for how I learn. I don't need to apologize for not having a degree. Especially working in the financial world—where degrees in accounting, finance, or economics are often assumed—I've had to work harder to earn trust. I've sat in meetings with bankers, auditors, and tax professionals who scanned my résumé for credentials I didn't have. I've sat across from millionaires and coached them through financial decisions, growth strategies, and business plans. I've learned to navigate complex audits, manage compliance, and lead high-level financial conversations—not because of a formal education, but because of hands-on experience, integrity, and God-given discernment. I've built a successful company with God's wisdom and grace. I've provided jobs for others. I don't need a framed degree to prove my value.

In 2012, I was accepted into the Goldman Sachs 10,000 Small Businesses program through Delgado College in New Orleans. This program is offered through Goldman Sachs foundation to help small business owners learn business fundamentals. It is a crash course in all things business but it's perfect because the curriculum is all hands-on and based on your business. It was collaborative, and great for how I learn. It gave me confidence in spaces that once intimidated me. In 2019, I also earned my fraud investigator certification after completing a week-long, in-person training. And in 2023, I passed a real estate course on my first try—all because it was taught using acronyms and stories.

Now in my 40s, I finally see my dyslexia not as a setback but as a strength. I think differently. I connect dots others might not see. Roughly 1 in 5 people have dyslexia, and major corporations are now recognizing its value.

In fact, many companies are beginning to shift their perspective—no longer viewing dyslexia as a barrier but as an asset. Major organizations have led the way specifically including dyslexia in their diversity strategies. These companies aren't just accommodating dyslexic individuals—they are actively seeking them out. Why? Because dyslexic thinkers often bring creativity, pattern recognition, strategic thinking, and problem-solving skills that can't be taught in a textbook.

What used to be considered a disadvantage is now being reframed as a unique advantage. Some employers are even implementing recruitment practices and workplace environments that are intentionally supportive of neurodiverse candidates. In doing so, they're not just filling a quota—they're expanding the way they think about innovation, leadership, and team strength.

It's incredibly validating to know that the very wiring of my brain—the thing I once saw as my biggest hurdle—is now something businesses are celebrating. Dyslexia isn't just something I've overcome. It's something I bring to the table. A 2018 report by Made by Dyslexia found that over 35% of U.S. Entrepreneurs are dyslexic.

I'm proud to be among them. I'm thankful for the teachers who saw me, the programs that met me where I was, and the grit God has given me. I may not have a degree, but I have a legacy of resilience, creativity, and growth. And most importantly, I've found hope—not in perfection, but in grace. In the messy middle of uncertainty, God was writing a redemptive story. He was showing me that hope is not found in a flawless record, but in His faithfulness through every flawed season.

As Paul writes in 2 Corinthians 12:9: *"But he said to me, 'My grace is sufficient for you, for my power is made perfect in weakness.' Therefore I will boast all the more gladly about my weaknesses, so that Christ's power may rest on me."*

Looking back, I see God's hand all over my education. He placed me in the right school, with the right teacher, at the right time. When I didn't even know what I needed—He did. And that's where the first sparks of hope began to flicker—hope that I wasn't forgotten, that I wasn't broken, that I was being uniquely prepared.

When the Body Fails but God Sustains

While dyslexia challenged me mentally and emotionally, in 2014, I faced a different battle—this time, a physical one.

I had always been athletic, playing basketball, volleyball, and running track during the years I was in school. But by 2014, after having two children, I began experiencing intense, unexplained pain. My entire body felt like it was on fire. My hips and pelvis ached constantly. Sitting, standing, or lying down— nothing brought relief. No amount of Biofreeze, massage, physical therapy or ice helped.

I saw my primary care doctor several times when he finally referred me to a rheumatologist. I had heard of rheumatologists, mostly in the context of elderly patients with arthritis, so I was hesitant but scheduled it.

After 6 months of intense pain I saw an amazing rheumatologist. He mentioned rheumatoid arthritis or a condition I'd never heard of—Ankylosing Spondylitis (AS). Though my blood work didn't clearly support it based on a positive gene marker, MRIs showed inflammation consistent with AS.

AS is a rare autoimmune disease that affects the spine and sacroiliac joints, sometimes causing the spine to fuse over time. At that time my doctor told me it affects less than 1% of the population. There is no cure—just pain management and treatments to slow progression.

I left that appointment with something I had desperately longed for—an answer. But I also carried a heavy truth: I had an autoimmune disease with no cure. The treatments were lifelong pain management and possibly moving to injectable biologics to prevent my spine from fusing. Was this really what I was facing in my early thirties?

I was discouraged. I felt defeated. I was sad and somewhat fearful. But, even in the midst of all this pain and bad news God provided an incredible doctor who has allowed me to bring all my questions and work as holistically as possible for my body while still supporting me medically.

Over the past 11 years, I've managed this condition with chiropractic care, diet changes, anti-inflammatory supplements, and regular stretching. I've stayed off injectables so far, but I trust that if I ever need them, God will give me peace in that step.

Some days are still hard. There are weeks I feel exhausted, flared up, or discouraged. But I've prayed three consistent prayers: for strength to endure, patience for progress, and courage to live fully. God has answered each one.

Psalm 73:26 reminds me: *"My flesh and my heart may fail, but God is the strength of my heart and my portion forever."*

In the Bible, we see this kind of grace in the story of Moses. A man who doubted his speaking ability and yet led a nation. Or in the life of Paul, who pleaded for God to remove a "thorn in the flesh" and was told instead that God's grace was enough. These stories remind me that weakness doesn't disqualify us. It draws us nearer to the One who makes us strong.

And perhaps most powerfully, in the story of the woman with the issue of blood in Luke 8, we see a picture of physical suffering paired with relentless hope. For twelve years, she battled a chronic condition. She had spent everything she had seeking answers—yet hope led her to reach out to Jesus. That one touch changed everything. Her healing didn't begin with wholeness. It began with faith—faith fueled by hope.

A Word for the Reader

Are you walking through pain right now—whether physical, emotional, or spiritual? Are you carrying a burden that feels too heavy to name? Maybe you feel like you've fallen behind, or that your limitations are louder than your strengths. If that's you, I want you to know—you are not alone.

What I've learned through every diagnosis, every setback, every unanswered question, is this: God is present in it all. Hope isn't the absence of struggle. Hope is the assurance that God is with you *in* the struggle.

If you're in a place where you feel stuck or discouraged, here are a few steps to begin finding hope again:

1. Acknowledge the pain – Don't minimize it. Name it. God can handle your honesty. Acknowledge the frustration, fear, anger, or sadness. Be real and honest with yourself about how you feel. The pain doesn't have to be physical—it can be emotional, mental, or even spiritual. Often, it's the internal battles that need the most attention. God sees it all, and He welcomes your truth.

2. Talk to someone you trust – Whether it's a friend, mentor, counselor, or pastor—let someone walk with you. Once you have named what you feel, tell someone about it so they can pray for you, encourage you and be with you through it.

3. Get still – Life moves fast, and when we're hurting, it's tempting to stay busy so we don't have to feel. But healing often begins in stillness. Set aside time to be quiet—without distractions. Rest. Let God speak. His voice is often clearest when we turn down the noise.

4. <u>Look back</u> – Think about the last time you made it through something hard. What did you learn? How did God show up? Let those past victories remind you that you're more resilient than you feel right now—and that God has never stopped being faithful. This is where journaling can come in handy. Journal the pain and journal the victories so that you can look back and see where He has brought you from.

5. <u>Cling to Scripture</u> – Let verses like Psalm 34:18 (*"The Lord is close to the brokenhearted"*) or Romans 15:13 (*"May the God of hope fill you with all joy and peace...as you trust in Him"*) anchor your spirit. This is often the time we feel like reading the bible the least. Don't let the devil win! Open your bible and write down some scripture then speak it out and let it encourage you.

6. <u>Move your body and care for your soul</u> – When you're discouraged, even basic self-care feels impossible. But go for a short walk, sit on the back porch and pray, drink a glass of water, take a deep breath, or play worship music. These small things are not shallow—they're practical things that can help shift your focus off your problem.

And if you can, take one small step today toward hope. Maybe it's getting out of bed. Maybe it's writing down what you're grateful for. Maybe it's simply whispering, "God, I need You."

Hope grows slowly, but it is never out of reach. Even now, in your hardest moments, God is planting seeds that will bloom in time. You may not see the fruit yet, but it is coming. Your story is not over. You are not forgotten. You are not behind. You are not broken beyond repair.

You are seen. You are held. And with God, you are being made whole—one step, one prayer, one breath at a time.

So keep going. Keep showing up. Keep pressing forward, even if it's just by inches. God's grace is sufficient, and His power is made perfect in your weakness.

I still have pain. I still have dyslexia. But I also have a purpose. I have grace. I have hope. And I have the kind of resilience that only grows through walking hand-in-hand with God through trial.

Not despite it—but because of it.

Chapter 11

Reflections in the Wilderness

I had always heard seasoned leaders and heartfelt pastors talk about being "in the wilderness." Their testimonies were laced with phrases like *deep sorrow* or *intense sadness*, or a dull ache that refused to lift. Sometimes the stories were tethered to depression, grief, or the shattered aftermath of unexpected upheaval. Whenever they spoke, the wilderness sounded like a place one barely crawled out of—a painful, crushing detour on the journey of life, the stretch of highway everyone hopes to bypass but few actually do.

I remember listening with polite empathy yet inward skepticism. I would quietly wonder—and if I'm honest, sometimes judge—*How can someone who knows God, trusts Him, and walks with Him end up in such a dark place? Were they exaggerating? Was the whole thing a figure of speech, some metaphor preachers used when attendance was low and they needed a tear-jerker of a sermon?*

To be fair, I've always been a glass-overflowing kind of girl. I'm the friend who turns detours into spontaneous photo ops, the mom who packs an extra bag of snacks "just in case," and the perpetual optimist who finds beauty in airport layovers and DMV lines. Chaos feels like an invitation to adventure; waiting becomes a chance to people-watch; and I can laugh at most things, including myself. So the notion that a sincere follower of Christ could remain stuck in sorrow—true, bone-deep sorrow—felt foreign to me.

My walk with Jesus has been lifelong. My earliest memories include felt-board Bible stories, whispered bedtime prayers, and worship songs drifting from the kitchen radio. Faith was my first language. I've never experienced a crisis of belief—not because I'm spiritually superior, but because Jesus captured my heart so early that leaving Him never felt like an option. My life has not been pain-free, but I have always held an unshakeable conviction: God is for me, God is with me, and God is endlessly good.

I adore Him—truly. If every language on earth and every note in heaven were at my disposal, they still wouldn't be enough to describe my gratitude for a Savior who loves me at my worst and lifts me when I cannot lift myself. My story is stitched together with testimonies—moments when His hand protected me, even from myself, and times His voice broke through noise and confusion to set my feet on solid ground.

A Slow-Motion Descent

That's what made this wilderness different. I'd weathered difficult seasons before, but this one arrived like dawn rather than a storm—slow and subtle. Think of the preheat cycle on an oven or the gradual stretch of morning light. There was no single dramatic blow, no headline-worthy tragedy. Instead, a series of gentle but relentless shifts unfolded until I woke up and realized the landscape of my life looked nothing like the map I'd been following.

It started when my husband retired from a twenty-year military career. For two decades we had lived by the "hurry up and wait" rhythm of service life. The calendar was never truly ours, and the next relocation hung over every long-term plan. Then, suddenly, we had choices—*too many* choices. What we had prayed for as "freedom" felt strangely disorienting. The scaffolding that had propped up our schedule, our community, and even parts of our identity was gone, and the wide-open sky felt less like possibility and more like vertigo.

Around the same time, the career plan I had labored toward—a path I sincerely believed God had scripted—began to unravel. I had prayed over it, invested years of study, dollars, and heartbeats. It felt like the culmination of so many obedience's strung together. Yet one quiet door after another clicked shut. They didn't slam; they whispered *no*. A soft, steady *no* is sometimes harder to accept than a loud one because it leaves you standing in a well-lit hallway, staring at a closed door, tempted to believe you misheard God entirely.

Then came an even stranger instruction: I sensed the Lord asking me to lay down something I had built with blood, sweat, and holy tears—work that was fruitful and meaningful and tightly woven into how people saw me and, if I'm honest, how I saw myself. Letting it go felt like handing over part of my own reflection. Yet obedience often precedes understanding, and surrender is rarely convenient.

The final blow was relational. A group of close friends—family by choice—accepted positions that would move them across the country. These were not casual acquaintances. These were the friends who knew the embarrassing, unfiltered middle of my stories, the ones who had keys to my house and opinions about my spaghetti recipe. We had dreamed about raising our children together, serving in church as a team, perhaps launching ministries side by side. Their departure wasn't a simple goodbye; it was the quiet collapse of a future I thought was certain.

Any one of these shifts would have been heavy. Together they stacked like stones on my chest: quiet grief, disoriented purpose, deferred dreams. With each change I felt another thread in my tapestry loosen, and soon the entire fabric quivered. Without realizing it, I wandered into a soul-desert. Days blurred like watercolor on wet paper. I kept parenting, working, attending Sunday service, singing on the worship team, but my joy evaporated. Life lost its saturation; I saw the world in muted grays. I wasn't angry at God, and I wasn't in active rebellion—I was just *distant*.

The Shattered Mirror

One night a dream startled me awake. In it, a large mirror toppled from a wall and shattered into a thousand jagged pieces. I lay beneath the glass, pinned by the weight of the fragments, peering through gaps, able to see light but unable to move toward it. Oddly, I wasn't afraid. A calm whisper drifted through the scene: *Do not struggle to escape. I will make this whole in My time.* I woke with the words echoing in my chest.

Mirrors are fascinating—solid until the instant they are not. When they break, the damage isn't a single crack; it's a constellation of fractures. Each shard still reflects light, but alignment is lost. That image lodged inside me because I felt like that mirror: still reflecting but fractured; still me, but misaligned.

For eighteen months I lived in that wilderness season. During that time, God never left me. He was quieter than I was used to, but He remained. He whispered through Scripture verses that leaped off the page during morning coffee. He nudged me with lyric lines in worship songs I sang even when enthusiasm failed. He wooed me with sunrises on days I questioned His timing.

And always there was the sense that something was being prepared, that the desert was not a punishment but a classroom.

One afternoon, while folding laundry, I sensed Him speak as clearly as my own thoughts: *This journey won't be fun, but it is necessary. There is more I have for you, and without this wandering you will never see it.* The statement jarred me, and immediately my mind scrolled through biblical accounts of wilderness   people.

- Hagar flashed across my memory. Banished with her young son, she wandered in the wilderness of Beersheba until her water ran out. She laid Ishmael under a bush, stepped back so she wouldn't watch him die, and sobbed. Yet "*God heard the boy crying,*" and an angel directed her to a hidden well (Genesis 21). The wilderness became the stage where God revealed Himself to her as El Roi—the God who sees.

- Elijah came next. After calling down fire on Mount Carmel, he outran a chariot, but Queen Jezebel's threat sent him fleeing. Under a solitary broom tree, Elijah begged God to end his life (1 Kings 19). Instead, God sent an angel with food and water, then met Elijah in a still, small voice on Mount Horeb. The prophet's exhaustion and fear were tended in that desolate space.

- David spent years dodging Saul in caves before becoming king. John the Baptist's pulpit was the Judean wilderness, and his diet was as sparse as his surroundings. And, of course, Jesus Himself was *"led by the Spirit into the wilderness"* for forty days, confronting temptation with the truth of Scripture (Matthew 4).

Over and over, the pattern emerges: the desert is not divine neglect; it is divine strategy. The wilderness is where identity is refined, distractions burn away, and reliance on God becomes visceral. *Preparation, not punishment.*

Knowing that didn't erase my grief, but it reframed it. I began to treat the fog as an instructor rather than an enemy. On days when prayer felt like reciting facts, I prayed anyway. When reading my Bible felt mechanical, I still opened the pages, believing the words were alive even when my heart felt numb.

The Closet-Floor Cathedral

My walk-in closet became a secret sanctuary. When the background noise of children's needs and unmet deadlines crescendoed, I would slip away, close the door, and lie on the floor. Sometimes I cried until no tears remained. Sometimes I simply listened for a heartbeat that wasn't my own. Every time

I emerged lighter, as if God had exchanged my sandbags for helium.

One seemingly ordinary Tuesday, while sautéing vegetables, the familiar heaviness rose. I turned off the stove mid-sizzle, whispered, "I need a minute," and retreated to my closet. As soon as my back hit the carpet, an inner vision unfolded. I saw myself in a dense forest, slumped against the base of a massive tree. My limbs felt heavy, my mouth dry—but when I looked up, sunlight pierced the canopy in brilliant columns, dust motes sparkling like confetti in the beams. In that golden hush, two Scriptures slid into focus:

- "The Lord Himself goes before you and will be with you; He will never leave you nor forsake you" (Deuteronomy 31:8).

- "See, I am doing a new thing! Now it springs up; do you not perceive it?" (Isaiah 43:19).

Warmth radiated through my body. I knew something had shifted. I was no longer merely surviving the wilderness; I was being led out of it. The terrain was still unfamiliar, but I could sense the tree line ending somewhere ahead.

Footsteps Toward the Clearing

The changes were incremental. I would wake with a verse humming in my spirit or notice color returning to landscapes that had seemed monochrome. Small opportunities opened— new friendships, fresh ideas, creative spark on projects I had shelved. None of it was flashy, but it was undeniably life.

Looking back, I see how God orchestrated a slow entry into the wilderness so that I would not be crushed by a sudden descent. He prepared me, just as He prepared manna for the Israelites: one day's portion at a time. Even when I could not feel His nearness, His Word remained a lamp to my feet and a light to my path (Psalm 119:105).

The wilderness required daily choice. I did not always feel hopeful, but I chose hope. I sometimes doubted my usefulness, but I chose obedience. I rarely understood the timetable, but I chose trust. Those choices became spiritual muscle memory, habits of dependence that will serve me long after this chapter closes.

Why God Loves Deserts

Maybe that is why God loves deserts. From a distance they appear lifeless yet hidden in the sand are seeds waiting for one good rain. Isaiah calls that sudden blooming a *desert rose*. I have stood in literal deserts and watched tiny wildflowers dot the dunes after an unexpected drizzle—proof that beauty can hide for years and burst to life overnight. The wilderness of the soul works the same way. It buries gifts too heavy for crowded seasons, then coaxes them to sprout when space is finally available.

I can see them now in my own life: a deeper empathy for people walking through disappointment, a calmness that no longer needs fast answers, and a sturdier trust in the quiet character of God. These are not souvenirs you can purchase in convenience; they are grown, watered by tears, fertilized by unanswered questions, harvested in due time.

So if you find yourself where I was—staring at a closed door or lying under shards of a broken mirror—let me pass you a canteen for the journey:

1. Stay in the Word even when it feels dry. Manna looks ordinary until it sustains you.

2. Anchor to community even when you feel dull. Aaron and Hur held up Moses' arms when his strength failed.

3. Rest in the truth that God never wastes wilderness. He feeds His people with unexpected bread, leads them with fire by night and cloud by day, and brings water from unlikely places—sometimes even from rocks.

When you finally step out of the trees and into the clearing, stack a few stones of remembrance like Joshua did at the Jordan (Joshua 4). Give your children and your future self a monument that says, *"God met me here."* Because one day someone you love will begin their own trek into barren land, and they will need evidence that streams still flow in deserts and that mirrors, even shattered, can sparkle beneath the sun.

Blessed in the Breaking

Seasons shift. Forests that look dead in January explode with life in April. Dry riverbeds fill again after spring rain. And souls that feel abandoned bloom under the consistent kindness of God. I write these words freshly emerged from that dry place—still tender, still healing—but confident that the faithful One who led me in has also led me out.

Luke 1:45 has become a banner over my life: "Blessed is she who has believed that the Lord would fulfill His promises to her." I am blessed—not because all my prayers were answered the way I expected, but because God was present in the silence and powerful in the pause. I carry blessings and brokenness in the same body, and Jesus walks comfortably among both.

I no longer judge when I hear a pastor speak of a dry, barren wilderness season. The wilderness isn't a sign of spiritual failure—it's a badge earned. Not one we wear with pride, but with quiet reverence. It marks a time when we walked a little closer with God, not because we were strong, but because we had no strength left of our own. I see now that those who speak of such seasons are not confessing weakness—they are revealing the sacred soil where their roots grew deeper. I honor it now. I understand it. Because I carry my own wilderness badge too.

We do not have to enjoy the wilderness, but we do have to walk through it. And when we do—hand-in-hand with the Shepherd—the barren place becomes holy ground. We emerge brighter, refined, and more aligned with the Light. Even a bit broken, we still reflect His glory—piece by piece, ray by ray—like that shattered mirror catching sunlight and scattering it into wild, radiant mosaics.

Chapter 12

The Power of Prayer: Israel and Facing Fear

"Do not fear." It's one of the most repeated phrases in Scripture—appearing 365 times, one for every single day of the year. That's no coincidence. It's as if God knew we'd need a fresh reminder each morning that fear doesn't have the final say.

And yet, we often misunderstand fear.

The Bible talks about two distinct types. The first is *Yirah*—a holy reverence, a trembling before something bigger than ourselves. It's the awe Moses felt standing barefoot before a burning bush. It's what you feel when you're summoned by name by a parent, and you *know* your practical joke backfired— your mom found out, your brother's angry, and your name echoing across the neighborhood carries the weight of coming consequences. It's not just terror—it's awe. It's a wake-up call that something serious, something sacred, is happening.

The second type is *Pachad*—a shadowy fear, often irrational, rooted in imagined futures. It's the fear that paralyzes. The anxiety that loops over and over again in our heads until it drowns out the truth. It's a lie wrapped in panic.

When Israel Calls

I had dreamed of going to Israel for years. It was more than just a bucket list item—it felt spiritual, like a desire placed in my heart by God Himself. I had reached a point in my relationship with God where I sensed there was so much more to learn, more to study, and I had only scratched the surface so far. I longed to see the places I had read about as a kid—the Sea of Galilee, the desert hills leading up to Mt. Nebo, all those stories I had heard. I knew there was so much more to understand about this book I had relied on for wisdom and foundational life principles from a very young age, like when I'd sit with the other kids in Sunday school, watching the teacher place Bible characters and little green trees on the gray felt board. But dreams like that can sit quietly in the background of life for years. For me, they were tucked behind layers of fear, practical limitations, and the constant refrain of "not now."

Israel was too expensive.

The timing was never right.

And worst of all—I was terrified to fly.

Then one day, it fell in my lap. A woman I'd met at a worship retreat the year before—a friend and mentor from afar who I finally got to know in real life—reached out. She was co-leading a study trip to Israel and was asking if I wanted to join.

Immediately, I felt the Lord say, *"This is the time."*

I didn't have every detail figured out. It wasn't convenient. Tensions were high between Israel and the surrounding countries, and neither my husband nor I, and our knowledge of what we saw on the news and his military background, felt it was the safest time to travel to the Middle East. But I knew that if I waited for perfect conditions, I'd never go. That was true in life—and especially in obedience.

So I said yes.

And something shifted.

Preparing in Faith (Not Fear)

Soon after I registered, two dear friends—bold, adventurous world travelers—told me they wanted to come too! That alone was an answered prayer. These were the kind of women who don't just bring fun; they bring courage. Their presence was God's provision in human form.

We met regularly over the following months. We prayed, dreamed, planned, and shopped. There was joy in the details— dinners out where we shared concerns and excitement, group Zoom calls where we met our kind, wise tour guide, and lists of all the must-haves we might need on the trip.

Early on, I felt the Lord speak something very specific to my heart: *"Don't study. Don't research. Don't read books. Just come with an open heart."* That was wildly out of character for me. I'm a planner, a reader, and a researcher. I generally will not do anything without knowing 100% about the good, bad and the ugly surrounding it and being completely prepared when walking into that situation. But as always God knew what He was doing.

He didn't want me arriving in Israel with preformed opinions or a checklist of expectations. He wanted me to walk in soft-hearted and curious, not pre-loaded with documentaries and historical footnotes. I'm so glad I obeyed that nudge.

Enter Fear: The Kind with Claws

As much as I was physically and mentally preparing, fear was beginning to bubble up—first slowly, then it seemed to hit all at once.

I've been afraid of flying since childhood. It's not just discomfort—it's dread. I get terribly motion sick, especially on airplanes. I catastrophize. I sweat through security lines and whisper frantic prayers at the gate. I have a deeply specific routine: I have to have two water bottles, calming essential oils - like lavender or peppermint. I must have certain sweet and salty snacks, gum, a magazine, a book or two, my bible and more—all packed with systematic purpose. My clothes are layered to account for any temperature shift between the cab rides to the hotels or the airplane rides themselves. Everything has to be just so for me to even function like a normal human being at an airport. It's like that scene in *Bridesmaids* when the woman sees a colonial woman on the wing of the plane and loses it—except in my case, I'm convinced the plane is going to nose-dive into the ocean at the slightest bump or change in elevation, even when we're not flying over water. Needless to say, it's a process of monumental proportions.

And this time, I wouldn't have my husband beside me to hold my hand like he normally had before. I would have to face this one differently and on my own.

About 7 months into the planning and 5 months before we were set to leave the dreams started.

I would dream almost nightly of plane crashes—terrifying scenarios where things went horribly wrong. It wasn't just the crash itself I feared, but everything that led up to it. There were engines sputtering out mid-flight, sudden malfunctions that sent the plane shaking violently, lights flickering and alarms blaring as I clutched my seat. In one dream, the oxygen masks dropped but didn't work. In another, the plane was on fire, and I could feel the heat creeping up my skin as we descended. There was one particularly vivid dream where we were crashing into the ocean, and as the water rushed in, I was trapped in the cabin, struggling to breathe, unable to escape. The sensation of drowning was so real I'd woke up gasping for air, heart pounding, drenched in sweat. And then, of course, there were the endless "what-ifs" in my waking life—what if the wing snaps off, what if a bird hits the engine, what if there's turbulence so severe we drop from the sky like a rollercoaster? My mind was relentless in concocting every worst-case scenario imaginable.

The fears didn't stop. They intensified.

To make it worse, videos and headlines of airline disasters started popping up constantly on my phone—completely unprovoked. It wasn't like I was searching for anything related to flights or accidents; these things just started appearing out of nowhere. It was as if someone (or maybe just my phone's algorithm) had decided to target my worst fears. I'd be scrolling through Instagram, trying to escape for a second, and there it was: a headline about a crash or a malfunction, with images of wreckage and emergency response teams. I'd move over to Facebook for some lighthearted posts, but no, the next thing I know, there's a news alert about a plane that caught on fire. It was as if the internet was mocking me. These videos weren't something I'd ever actively sought out, but they kept popping up—almost daily, it felt like. My social media feeds seemed like they were conspiring against me, intensifying my anxiety with every swipe and scroll. It was like I couldn't escape my fear, even in the digital world.

I hadn't told anyone what I was experiencing. And yet, fear was everywhere I looked. I was being targeted. Not by an algorithm, but by an enemy who saw an opening.

That's how the enemy works. He creeps in through cracks. He watches for wounds. He waits for us to get tired, distracted, and discouraged. Then he starts weaving confusion until all we can see is the thing we fear most.

And that's what happened to me.

I was exhausted. I couldn't sleep. I was spending time in the Word. I was praying, but I wasn't able to get the fear to stop. The anxiety was overwhelming. I started to wonder if these were warnings from God and not attacks at all. Should I cancel this trip altogether? Was He trying to tell me something?

More than once, I almost backed out. I convinced myself several times that this must be God warning me to stay home but something kept calling me to get there!

The D.C. Moment

Then something unexpected happened. I had to book a last-minute work trip to Washington, D.C. I bought the ticket, traveled to D.C. and realized—*I wasn't afraid.*

It hit me like a lightning bolt. *Why am I not afraid of this flight, but every time I think of Israel, I'm paralyzed?*

That was when it clicked.

This was warfare. This wasn't God warning me not to go. This was the enemy trying to stop something *God wanted me to experience.*

And I knew if the enemy was fighting this hard, it meant something *big* was waiting for me on the other side.

Asking for prayer doesn't come easily for me. It feels vulnerable—like I'm exposing a part of myself that I'd rather keep hidden, as if admitting I need help somehow makes me weak or needy. But I know this is something I need to work on. The Bible is clear about the importance of bringing our struggles into the light, and that when two or more are gathered in Jesus' name, He is there with us. So even though it's uncomfortable, I recognize that seeking prayer from others is not only necessary, but it's part of what God calls us to do.

In this instance God had made it clear: *You're not going to win this battle alone.*

So I told my friends. I told our trip leaders. I told my family. I told my church's prayer team and let them lay hands on me.

I called friends out of state.

I sat in living rooms with trusted sisters in Christ and prayed. We wept. We asked for a breakthrough.

I wrote out verses. Taped them up. Read them aloud every morning and every night:

- *"Fear not, for I am with you..."* (Isaiah 41:10)

- *"When I am afraid, I will trust in You..."* (Psalm 56:3)

- *"The Lord is my light and salvation—whom shall I fear?"* (Psalm 27:1)

I stopped watching the news. I deactivated social media. I created space for peace.

The anxiety didn't disappear overnight—but it shifted. The power it had over me started to break.

When the day came to fly, I was still nervous. My stomach churned. My body shook.

But I walked forward anyway while being encouraged each step of the way by my friends traveling with me.

And as I buckled into my seat on that plane, something sacred happened. The fear didn't win.

I felt a peace that surpassed understanding. And I slept the entire flight until the very last hour. While I did get sick I had my friend traveling with me and she supported me and helped take care of me and WE MADE IT!

That wasn't luck. That was grace.

The trip to Israel was life changing. I experienced the Lord in places I'd only read about—on the Sea of Galilee, in the Garden of Gethsemane, walking ancient paths worn by the feet of prophets and Jesus Himself. I saw one of the 7 wonders of the world in Jordan, Petra, an incredibly beautiful part of creation.

But none of that would have happened if I had let fear dictate my story.

Looking back, I can clearly see the enemy tried to steal this moment. He nearly succeeded. But prayer turned the tide. Prayer from friends. Prayer from mentors. Prayer from my own trembling lips.

And God responded.

Why Prayer Matters

Prayer is not just a comforting ritual. It's not an emotional release valve. It is power. It moves heaven and shakes the gates of hell.

I needed others to pray when I couldn't. I needed to borrow their strength. And God honored that.

We aren't made to fight our battles alone. We are designed to live in community—and that includes how we pray.

You might be reading this and facing a fear of your own. Maybe it's not flying. Maybe it's stepping into ministry, reconciling a broken relationship, or facing a diagnosis. Whatever it is, hear me:

> Sometimes, the bravest thing you can do is do it
> afraid knowing God is with you and He is for you!

Closing the Chapter with Faith

God didn't just get me through the flight; He redeemed the entire journey. Every moment of fear, every bit of anxiety, He transformed. When I stepped onto that plane, I wasn't just facing a flight across the world—I was facing a battle between my flesh and my faith. But in those hours, He poured peace into my soul. It wasn't a calm that came from the absence of fear, but a peace that came in the presence of it. I could feel His hand steadying me, holding me through every turbulence, every moment of panic that tried to take root in my mind.

He reminded me, in no uncertain terms, that obedience doesn't mean the absence of fear. It means moving forward anyway, even when the heart races and the doubts scream. It means stepping out, despite the inner chaos, trusting that He has a purpose in the discomfort. And prayer? Prayer is what makes that movement possible. It's the lifeline that connects us to His strength when we feel like we have none left.

In those moments, 2 Corinthians 12:9-10 echoed in my heart: *"My grace is sufficient for you, for my power is made perfect in weakness... For when I am weak, then I am strong."* I realized that in my weakness, I was actually more aligned with His power than ever before. I was weak but I wasn't alone.

I was afraid but I obeyed.

I did it trembling, with every ounce of courage I could muster, but I did it anyway. The fear was real, the anxiety still present, but so was His presence. And in that, I found my strength.

And you know what? God met me in the sky. He wasn't just with me in my quiet prayers on the ground; He was with me every mile of the flight, every shaky breath I took. He was right there, filling the space between my fear and my faith, reminding me that He is faithful, even in the most uncertain moments.

What are you up against today where fear is making it impossible to see through? I encourage you to close the social media, text a friend and ask them to pray for you, open your bible and see how the power of scripture can bring a peace that will surpass all understanding for you. I believe He is drawing you close to him to gain freedom from your fear today!

Chapter 13

More Than Rescue: Receiving the Goodness of God

Sharing the joyful moments of our lives—the breakthroughs, the blessings, the victories—can sometimes feel like walking a tightrope. There's a tension we carry, a quiet fear that our celebration might be mistaken for insensitivity. In a world where so many are walking through deep valleys, it can feel risky to speak from the mountaintop. We don't want to come across as boastful or unaware. So we often hold back, dimming our light—not out of pride, but out of caution, not wanting to invite judgment or cause further hurt.

But what if sharing our joy could become a source of hope for someone else?

As someone who's spent years navigating wilderness seasons, I understand the inner struggle. When I was in the trenches—grieving, healing, rebuilding—hearing someone else's story of joy could feel like salt in an open wound. But over time, I've learned that the light of someone else's testimony doesn't have to dim our own—it can guide us forward. Revelation 12:11 says, "They triumphed over him by the blood of the Lamb and by the word of their testimony." Our stories matter. They help others overcome. And so, today, I share one of mine. If you're in a valley, may this be a lifeline of hope. If you're on a mountaintop, celebrate with me—and tuck this story into your heart for the days you need to believe again.

I was in a good place—a season marked by peace, healing, and a quiet kind of joy. Life wasn't perfect, but it felt steady, anchored. I was waking up each morning with purpose, often pausing in the stillness to whisper, "Thank You, Lord." There were moments when I would simply look around and think, *This is good.* Not flawless. Not without its own effort or pain. But undeniably good.

These moments hit differently when you know what it's like to live in the dark. I remembered the years of addiction, abusive relationships, emotional wreckage, and the pit of self-loathing I had crawled out of. I remembered the long nights, the shattered pieces, and the whispered prayers when I wasn't sure I'd make it another day. But God. His grace met me there. He didn't just rescue me—He restored me.

In the fall of 2023, I listened to a church message about the importance of having a bucket list—not just as a fun thing, but as a faith builder. The pastor encouraged us to dream with God, to write down desires, goals, even the things that seemed impossible or just plain silly. It was like he was telling me, believe because you never know what He will do!

I sat there pondering, reflecting on how many items I had already seen God fulfill: becoming a mom and a wife, starting my own business, living near the beach and traveling to Israel. Dreams I had once only whispered in passing had become part of my reality. And still, I wondered, *What now?* What could I possibly dream up next?

So, I started writing. I added things like "travel to Europe," "record original music," "go on a family mission trip." And then, just for fun—and a little bit in jest—I scribbled: *sing at Carnegie Hall.* I laughed at myself. I mean, really? It felt way too far-fetched, way too extravagant but when you're thinking about wild, far-fetched dreams, that one fit right in for me. For a musician, Carnegie Hall isn't just a venue; it's a symbol. It's the kind of place you read about in music history books, where legends have stood under the spotlight and poured their hearts into the silence. It's not just a performance—it's a milestone, a statement. To sing or play there is to be counted among the best, to add something unforgettable to your artistic story. The pastor's words rang in my ears: *Add the impossible. Watch what God does.* So, with a mix of amusement and curiosity, I added it: "singing at Carnegie Hall."

With that, I tucked the idea away in my mind.

A few months later, my husband and I were driving home on a dreary, rainy day when a text popped up on my phone from a close friend—who also happens to be my voice coach. To this point, the Carnegie Hall dream had stayed between God and me. I hadn't told a soul. But there it was, blinking on my screen: "I have an opportunity for you. Performing with Kari Jobe and Cody Carnes at Carnegie Hall. Thoughts?"

I stared at it for a moment. I didn't answer right away. My heart raced. The same heart that had dared to dream now pounded in disbelief. I felt the Holy Spirit whisper, *See? I saw you. I heard you. And I remembered.*

Just a few months earlier, I had been questioning everything about my music journey—whether to continue leading worship, whether to write and record music, whether it truly was part of my purpose. I had prayed, asking for clarity, for confirmation. Carnegie Hall had been my silent fleece: "If you want me to keep doing this, show me in a way that only You could." And here it was—this far-fetched dream was becoming an opportunity that no one else knew I wanted, delivered straight to my inbox.

I said yes. And as I did, I felt God's delight—like a proud father watching His daughter open the gift she'd been too afraid to ask for. He told me He was opening an impossible door to show me that even the seemingly trivial desires of our hearts matter to Him because of His love for us. It was a gift to me; packaged from Him.

But just because something is a gift doesn't mean it comes without a fight.

The journey to Carnegie Hall was layered with challenges: travel logistics, finances, coordinating life back home, and facing one of my long-standing battles—my fear of flying.

Flying has long been a source of anxiety for me. As I shared in an earlier chapter, I first became fully aware of the depth of that fear during my trip to Israel early in 2023. In the weeks leading up to that flight, I faced intense spiritual warfare—nightmares, panic attacks, sleepless nights, and an overwhelming sense of dread. Looking back, I now recognize it for what it truly was: a targeted attempt by the enemy to keep me from a part of the journey that would stretch my faith, deepen my dependence on God, and ultimately lead to greater spiritual growth.

The same thing happened before Carnegie Hall. Fear crept in again—same anxiety, same unrest. But this time, I was prepared. I had tools, prayer warriors, and a strengthened spirit. I knew I had the choice to either partner with fear or partner with God.

So I boarded that plane—scared but obedient. I reminded myself of the truth in Matthew 19:26: *"With man this is impossible, but with God all things are possible."* Not some things. ALL things. Even peace for a fearful traveler.

And just like in Israel, once I landed, the fear lifted. It was like the enemy's grip broke the moment I stepped into obedience.

Not only was I free from fear, but I was filled with a quiet power—I had done it afraid. And God had carried me through.

These trips revealed something important: the enemy often aims for our most vulnerable places. For me, fear of flying has been one of those areas. But rather than give in and cancel my plans, I chose to stand firm in faith. I leaned on God's strength, trusting that His power was greater than anything I was up against. Overcoming fear and anxiety hasn't been a one-time victory—it's an ongoing journey. While God delivered me years ago from needing medication for anxiety, I still encounter moments where those emotions rise up. In those times, I cling to the truth of Matthew 19:26: *"With man this is impossible, but with God all things are possible."* My feelings don't determine the outcome—God's faithfulness does.

Saturday was filled with rehearsals and preparation. Kari and Cody were just as kind and humble as you'd hope they'd be. They ministered with a purity and reverence that was contagious. Our choir team was a beautiful picture of unity—strangers quickly becoming friends, all brought together by a shared desire to worship with excellence.

That night, I fell asleep with a heart full of anticipation. And then, Sunday came.

I woke to soft sunlight streaming through the hotel blinds, and for a second, it felt like a dream. But then it hit me: *Today is the day.*

As we stepped out into the cold, crisp New York air, I could feel the energy in the city—bustling, alive, full of promise. We walked through the backstage door of Carnegie Hall, winding through quiet corridors and up stairwells until we reached the choir room. It was a buzz with each choir member finding a spot to place their belongings, some doing their hair or touching up their makeup, others warming up their voices and the rest of them chatting with excitement of what the day would be like.

Then, we lined up and headed toward the stage. One by one, we stepped out from behind the red velvet curtain.

I'll never forget that moment—the first look from the stage. With every step, you could hear the collective gasp as choir members took in the awe-inspiring view. The majestic beauty. It's beautiful history gleaming and dating back to the 1800's. Each of us recalled all of the greats who had stood on this stage before us and reveled in the fact we were standing where Tchaikovsky conducted on opening night. The same stage where Frank Sinatra and The Beatles performed. The place where, for hundreds of years, legends' notes had bounced off the perfectly balanced acoustic walls, only to land on the tips of the audience's ears, creating a breathtaking display of music at its finest. Even Kari Jobe, upon her arrival, stood there in tears, overcome by the significance of it all.

The concertgoers began to file in, their footsteps echoing softly through the grand hall as they found their seats. The rustle of programs, the low hum of conversation filled the space with a quiet energy. I watched from my choir seat behind the string instruments, my heart swelling as I spotted familiar faces—family members, friends, and strangers alike—making their way into the audience. Some waved from the balconies with eager smiles, their excitement radiating even from a distance. Others sat in still awe, taking in the architectural beauty of Carnegie Hall, their eyes lifting to the ornate ceilings and gilded edges as if to take a mental snapshot of the moment.

There was a sacred kind of hush that settled just before the lights dimmed, the kind of stillness that only comes when anticipation and reverence meet. It was as if the room itself was holding its breath, waiting for what was to come. Every seat filled, every voice quieted, and every heart leaned in.

The lights softened, casting a golden glow across the stage as the first notes swelled through the air. Then, the moment everyone had been waiting for arrived.

Cody Carnes stepped out first, sharp and composed in a classic black tuxedo. He carried himself with quiet confidence and humility, the kind that commands respect without asking for it. His presence, grounded and sincere, set the tone—this wasn't a performance; it was worship.

Moments later, Kari Jobe emerged, and it felt as if the room exhaled in awe. She floated across the stage in a breathtaking blush pink gown that billowed around her like petals unfolding in bloom. The fabric shimmered subtly under the lights, catching movement with each graceful step. She moved with the elegance of a princess and the peace of someone who knew she was walking in divine purpose. Her face was radiant—not with makeup or lights—but with the unmistakable joy of the Lord.

Together, they stood beneath the towering arch of Carnegie Hall's historic stage—not as celebrities, but as vessels. Vessels prepared to pour out praise, to usher in the presence of God in a place that had witnessed musical greatness but now would be filled with glory.

It was holy. It was beautiful. And it was just beginning.

From the very first note, it felt like heaven met earth.

The symphonic instruments swelled in perfect unity—strings, brass, percussion—all rising like a wave of praise. The band gave rhythm and depth, and the choir's harmonies wrapped the room in rich, sacred sound. It wasn't just music—it was worship. A holy offering.

Kari's voice lifted, pure and anointed, carrying the lyrics like a prayer. Cody joined her, their voices blending as one, not performing but leading us into the presence of God. The audience responded—not as spectators, but as worshipers.

Hands raised, eyes closed, tears falling. It was a moment where the ordinary became infused with the divine.

We closed with "The Blessing," declaring God's favor over generations. As the music faded and the lights softened, a hush fell over the room.

Then came the final song, "Amen"—sung acapella, hundreds of voices in perfect harmony. No instruments. Just hearts lifted together in worship. The sound echoed into stillness, reverent and raw.

I closed my eyes and thought, this must be what worship sounds like in heaven.

Even now, I get chills remembering it.

As the final note faded and we stepped off the stage, I carried more than just a memory—I carried a revelation. What had unfolded wasn't just a once-in-a-lifetime experience or a dream come true. It was something deeper, more personal.

This wasn't a story of hardship. It wasn't a rescue mission. It was a reminder. A reminder that God isn't just in the business of getting us out of hard places—He's in the business of gifting us good ones.

Psalm 37:4 says, *"Delight yourself in the Lord, and He will give you the desires of your heart."* He didn't say He'd only give you the spiritual ones, or the noble ones. He sees every desire—even the ones we're afraid to ask for.

I believe that when I added "Carnegie Hall" to my list, God smiled. Like a dad at Christmas, watching His child open the very thing they'd dreamed of all year. I bet He thought, *wait 'til she sees this. After everything she's been through, I can't wait to watch her light up.*

It's easy to downplay the little dreams, the fun dreams, the "trivial" ones. But faith grows when we give God access to our full heart—not just our needs, but our wants. And when He answers those prayers—especially the ones we know we couldn't accomplish on our own—our trust deepens.

This gift became a deposit in my faith account. Something I can withdraw from during the next storm. If financial trouble hits or when health challenges arise, I'll look back and say, *If God opened Carnegie Hall for me, why wouldn't He do another miracle now?*

If you're in a season of waiting, I want to encourage you: Keep dreaming. Keep asking. Keep adding the "silly" things to your list. Because God is a good Father, and He delights in blessing His children—not just with what they need to survive, but with what brings them joy.

Ephesians 3:20 reminds us, *"Now to Him who is able to do immeasurably more than all we ask or imagine..."* More than we ask. More than we imagine. That's the God we serve.

This trip reminded me that He's not just my rescuer—He's also my rewarder and His goodness doesn't stop at deliverance. It overflows into delight.

So write the list. Add the dreams. Ask for the impossible.

Because with God, all things truly are possible.

Take a few quiet moments to dream with God. What desires—big or small—have you tucked away or deemed too impossible? Write them down. Even the ones that feel silly, far-off, or too fragile to voice aloud. Then, invite God into them. Trust that He not only hears you but delights in giving good gifts to His children.

Ask yourself:

- What would I ask for if I truly believed God wanted to bless me?

- Where have I limited God to only rescuing me instead of rewarding me?

- How can I begin to hope again—boldly, audaciously, faithfully?

Now take one step—no matter how small—toward believing again. God is not just your deliverer. He's also the giver of joy, and the author of impossible dreams come true.

Chapter 14

Living on Purpose

As we come to the final stretch of this journey, I invite you to pause and breathe. You have walked with me through valleys of pain, unearthed buried wounds, and confronted the hard truths of trauma. But we've also witnessed the slow and sacred work of healing—of being pieced back together by grace. As the dust begins to settle, a question rises from the rubble: *What now?* Healing was never meant to be the end of the story—it's the beginning.

This chapter is about stepping into purpose, not as a final destination, but as a daily choice. It's about learning to live from a place of connection—first to God, then to others, and finally, to ourselves. When our spirit, mind, and body are in alignment, we don't just survive—we thrive. Purpose gives meaning to our healing and turns our pain into something powerful: a life lived with intention, impact, and deep-rooted peace.

Rediscovering God as Our Source

Before anything else, we must understand that true purpose begins with God. We were created on purpose, for a purpose. Our identity is not rooted in what we do but in *whose* we are. In a world that pressures us to define ourselves by titles, achievements, and appearances, it's vital to return to our creator.

Practical Step 1: Establish a Daily Connection with God (Build the habit)

- Start each day with a quiet moment of prayer, reading scripture or focusing on some worship music. This doesn't have to be lengthy or complicated, over time God will create space and time for you to grow in this but start small to build the habit. Even five minutes of focused attention on God's presence can ground your day in truth.

- Consider reading a Psalm, writing a short prayer, listening to a study on the bible app or simply sitting in silence with God to start to turn your ear toward His voice. We often do not feel comfortable with silence. I remember when this was weird for me but the Bible tells us in 1 Kings 19:12, after an earthquake and a fire, God's presence is revealed not in those powerful displays, but in a still small voice. How do we expect to hear God amidst the noise of the world if we do not slow down, pause and listen? Over time as we settle our minds and cut out the noise he will begin to speak to us and encourage us, we just have to slow down long enough to hear.

Reminder: Purpose flows from presence. When you are connected to the One who made you, you gain clarity about why you were made.

The Power of People

Healing is deeply personal, but it was never meant to be solitary. We are wired for connection. From the Garden of Eden, God said it wasn't good for man to be alone. Community not only supports us in pain but also fuels our purpose. The people in your life can speak truth, offer perspective, and encourage you to keep going when you feel lost.

Practical Step 2: Cultivate Meaningful Relationships

- Intentionally invest in healthy relationships that reflect mutual love, honesty, and encouragement. Join a small group, reach out to a mentor, or simply schedule regular time with a trusted friend. Vulnerability is the soil where authentic connection grows.
- Don't wait for people to reach out to you, take the initiative to be their friend and connect with them. Busy people are lonelier than we think and oftentimes I think

we use what we see as their busy life on social media as an excuse to not invite them to coffee or lunch. Reach out and connect, plant the seed. God made us for a healthy connection. If you have lunch and nothing comes of it, do it again. Get to know them, ask them their story. I have never met someone who did not have an incredible story. I am not saying be the only giver in the relationship but start to build and cultivate the relationship and as you reach out in faith to do that God will bring the right people into your life at just the right time for you and for them.

- Read books and listen to podcasts about boundaries and healthy relationships so that you can become a better friend and communicator.

Reminder: Isolation can feel safe, but healing requires community. Don't rob yourself of the joy and growth that comes from walking alongside others who also want to grow and become better and healthier versions of themselves.

The Role of the Mind

Our thoughts shape our lives. What we believe about ourselves, our past, and our future becomes the lens through which we interpret every single thing that we see or do. Trauma can distort our thinking, convincing us that we're unworthy, broken beyond repair, or incapable of real change. But renewing the mind is possible—and essential for living with purpose.

At just 16 years old, Dr. Edith Eger was imprisoned in Auschwitz along with her family. On the very first day, she stood in what prisoners called the "finger line"—a chilling moment when Nazi guards would silently point left or right. Left meant life. Right meant death. Edith watched in horror as her mother was pointed right, while she and her sister were sent to the left. Her mother was burned alive that day.

What followed were unspeakable horrors. But after liberation, Edith didn't allow the darkness to define her. She moved to the United States, earned a doctorate in psychology, and devoted her life to trauma healing.

Now 97, Dr. Eger is a renowned speaker and author whose books, including *The Choice*, guide readers through the process of healing from even the deepest wounds. Her message is clear: we cannot control what happens to us, but we can choose how we respond.

She writes, *"Your attitude is the key. The way you look at anything—as an opportunity. Auschwitz was my classroom."* That unspeakable place, she says, taught her the very tools she would later use to help others heal.

Perhaps her most liberating insight is this: *"Everything can be taken away from a human being except what they put in their mind. What happens to you is not your identity."*

Dr. Eger's life reminds us that healing is not about forgetting—it's about choosing to rise. Her story stands as a living testament to the power of mindset, choice, and the unbreakable strength of the human spirit.

Practical Step 3: Practice Thought Awareness and Renewal

- Start by identifying common negative thought patterns whether that is with a trusted friend, mentor or professional counselor. The depth to which you are willing to seek healing will be the depth God will meet you and provide the right people and circumstances along the way.
- When you catch yourself thinking, "I'm not enough," counter it with truth: "I am fearfully and wonderfully made" (Psalm 139:14). Write down affirmations rooted in Scripture and post them on your phone, on your bathroom mirror, beside your bed, on your computer at work. Soak them in when you have a bad phone call or rough conversation with a friend. Hide the word in your heart like it says in Psalm 119:1, "I have hidden your word in my heart that I might not sin against you." This talks about having the word in your memory and your heart so that in the moments we need to recall it we can.

Reminder: You don't have to accept every thought that enters your mind as truth. Through God's Word, you have both the strength and the spiritual tools to recognize and deflect the enemy's fiery darts of deception—and the power to renew your mind with what is true.

Caring for the Body

Our physical health is often the most neglected part of healing. Yet our bodies are temples of the Holy Spirit (1 Corinthians 6:19). When we care for our bodies, we honor God and equip ourselves to fulfill our purpose with energy and endurance. If we are not physically healthy that shows up in exhaustion, unhealthy patterns of eating, addiction to substances and overall unhappiness with our image which can lead to unhealthy mental patterns and thoughts as well.

Practical Step 4: Establish Rhythms of Physical Health Begin with small, sustainable habits:

- Choose nourishing foods that fuel you: Set aside an hour on the weekend to plan and prep your meals, so you're not caught off guard during the busyness of the week and tempted to make unhealthy choices. Build in flexibility—like a cheat meal or treat—so your routine feels sustainable, not restrictive.

- Prioritize sleep and hydration: Don't feel obligated to say yes to everything. Be intentional with your schedule and learn to say no to commitments that don't align with your purpose. Prioritizing rest and relaxation is essential to your overall health and well-being.
- Make regular movement a part of your routine, even if it's just a short walk or a few minutes of stretching. The focus isn't on perfection but on consistency: Start with a manageable goal—like a 10- to 20-minute walk each day or walking a mile three times a week—and intentionally schedule it into your calendar. Begin small and gradually increase your goal each month or quarter to keep it sustainable. You can make it more enjoyable by inviting a friend or family member to join you, or by listening to a sermon, a book or a podcast as you walk or run.

Reminder: Your body is not your enemy. It's a sacred vessel that carries the purpose God placed within you.

Living with Intention

Purpose isn't always about big dreams or grand accomplishments. It's found in the everyday moments—how you show up, how you love, how you respond. Living on purpose means waking up each day with the awareness that your life matters, and your choices ripple out further than you know.

Practical Step 5: Set Daily Intentions

- Each morning, ask yourself: "What kind of person do I want to be today?" Write down or verbalize one intention and one action that aligns with your values. Whether it's choosing patience with your child or courage in a conversation, these small acts add up to a purposeful life.
- Journal: You can do this daily, weekly, monthly.... just start. This can be such a great reminder in hard times of where you have come from and what you have overcome. It can also show you the prayers God has answered along the way. Lastly, it can be a lasting legacy for your kids or family to read after you are gone. It's something where they can see the real you, your struggles, your triumphs and your feelings you may have been too afraid to share while on earth.

Reminder: You won't always get it right, and that's okay. Grace covers your gaps, and growth is a process.

When You Lose Your Way

Even with the best intentions, there will be days you feel disconnected or discouraged. That doesn't mean you've failed. It means you're human. The key is to return and adjust the sails—again and again—to God, to your people, to your habits. Purpose is not about perfection; it's about persistence and intentionality.

You're doing the work either way—so ask yourself: Do you want the hard that heals, or the hard that kills?

Practical Step 6: Create a "Return" Plan

- When you feel off track, have a few go-to practices that ground you: a worship playlist, a walk in nature, journaling a prayer, or calling a trusted friend. Keep them accessible and use them without guilt or shame.
- Find a book, podcast or sermon that can fill you with encouragement or speak hope to you to pull you back onto the right track.

Reminder: You were never expected to walk this out alone. God walks with you, and He delights in your desire to live on purpose.

Final Encouragement

You are not the same person who began this journey. I am not the same person I was sitting on the steps of my childhood home wondering when I would see my dad again. I am not the same person who chose the wrong relationships that led to pain and trauma. You are not the same person that had that addiction or that family member hurt you. You have been called to be refined, strengthened, and freed. The pain that once felt like the end has been transformed into a foundation. And now, you can stand with a new perspective—not only healed but whole. And from this wholeness, you are called to live with purpose.

Let this be your charge: Stay connected. Stay open. Stay grounded. The world doesn't need a perfect version of you—it needs the real, healed, purposeful you.

You are here for a reason. Now go, and live like it.

About the Author

Hope Blankenship is a wife, mom of three, and deeply rooted woman of faith. Her family's journey—shaped by years of military life and now grounded in the rhythms of post-service living—has given her a deep understanding of resilience, transition, and purpose. These real-life experiences fuel her passion for helping others move from survival to discovering their purpose.

A natural entrepreneur, Hope is the founder, partner and CEO of To The Rescue Bookkeeping, a nationwide financial services firm offering bookkeeping, payroll, and consulting for small businesses. She also owns HB Coaching and Consulting, where she specializes in fraud investigation, operational strategy, and business process development. In addition, Hope is a licensed realtor on the Mississippi Gulf Coast, where she and her husband own and manage a portfolio of real estate properties.

Hope is a Certified Fraud Examiner (CFE), a QuickBooks ProAdvisor, and a proud graduate of the Goldman Sachs 10,000 Small Businesses Program. Her leadership and dedication have earned her several notable honors, including the SBA Young Entrepreneur of the Year for Mississippi and the Lifetime Achievement Volunteer Excellence Award at Keesler Air Force Base. Her bookkeeping firm, To The Rescue Bookkeeping, has also been recognized as one of the Top 50 Accounting Firms in the Nation for two consecutive years—an honor that reflects both her commitment to excellence and her heart for serving small businesses.

Beyond her professional accomplishments, Hope is a speaker, worship leader, and mentor who finds joy in encouraging women through their own faith and healing journeys. When she's not working or serving, you'll find her soaking up time with her family, reading a good book, walking the beach, discovering new places, enjoying good food, or singing and playing the piano. These everyday moments remind her that hope isn't just found after the storm—it's woven into the beauty of life itself.

Finding Hope is a reflection of that belief—a story of redemption, growth, and the faithfulness of God through every chapter of life.

Follow her on her blog at aboutthejourney.me for encouragement, practical tools for growth, and real-life stories that inspire hope and healing.

References

Beattie, M. (1987). *Codependent no more: How to stop controlling others and start caring for yourself*. Hazelden.

Biblica, Inc. (2011). *Holy Bible: New International Version (NIV)*. https://www.biblica.com

Blue Star Families. (2023). *Military family lifestyle survey*. https://bluestarfam.org

Cloud, H. (1992). *Changes that heal: Four practical steps to a happier, healthier you*. Zondervan.

Gaskins, T. (n.d.). You teach people how to treat you by what you allow... [Quote].

Journal of Family Psychology. (n.d.). Children's understanding of conflict and resolution in parental relationships [Study summary].

National Military Family Association. (n.d.). *Military spouse mental health statistics*. https://www.militaryfamily.org

Orther, C., & Rose, K. (2006). *Social support and military family adjustment to deployment*. *Journal of Military Family Research*, 5(2), 112–125.

Stansbury, L. (n.d.). "There is no pain so great as the memory of joy in present grief." [Quote].

Verywell Health. (n.d.). *What is emotional abuse?* https://www.verywellhealth.com/what-is-emotional-abuse-5209555

Unknown. (n.d.). "Love should not mean losing yourself." [Quote].

Eger, Edith Eva. *The Choice: Embrace the Possible*. New York: Scribner, 2017.

Scripture References

All Scripture is from the Holy Bible, New International Version®, NIV®. Copyright © 1973, 1978, 1984, 2011 by Biblica, Inc.™ Used by permission. All rights reserved worldwide.

www.ingramcontent.com/pod-product-compliance
Lightning Source LLC
Chambersburg PA
CBHW061747120626
46550CB00005B/1922